Social-Emotional Competences of Preschoolers:
The Impact of Outdoor Educational Activities

ERZIEHUNGSKONZEPTIONEN UND PRAXIS

EDUCATIONAL CONCEPTS AND PRACTICE

Edited by Gerd-Bodo von Carlsburg

VOLUME 84

PETER LANG

Otilia Clipa / Erica Cimpan

Social-Emotional Competences of Preschoolers: The Impact of Outdoor Educational Activities

PETER LANG

Bibliographic Information published by the Deutsche Nationalbibliothek
The Deutsche Nationalbibliothek lists this publication in
the Deutsche Nationalbibliografie; detailed bibliographic
data is available online at http://dnb.d-nb.de.

Library of Congress Cataloging-in-Publication Data
A CIP catalog record for this book has been applied for at the
Library of Congress.

ISSN 0723-7464
ISBN 978-3-631-80754-5 (Print)
E-ISBN 978-3-631-83912-6 (E-PDF)
E-ISBN 978-3-631-83913-3 (EPUB)
E-ISBN 978-3-631-83914-0 (MOBI)
DOI 10.3726/b17440

© Peter Lang GmbH
Internationaler Verlag der Wissenschaften
Berlin 2020
All rights reserved.

Peter Lang – Berlin · Bern · Bruxelles ·
New York · Oxford · Warszawa · Wien

This publication has been peer reviewed.

www.peterlang.com

Table of contents

Introduction

Today's society, facing a fast-forward transformation in the area of communication and the impact of technology in all areas of life, is distinguished by increasing aggression and decreasing the collaboration and teamwork and involvement in the social life of the community. Under these conditions, it is up to education to ensure the harmonious development of the human personality – with its real needs, both intellectual and emotional, and social – and its integration into a society that is constantly changing. The educator is asked to be himself developed emotionally and socially, and bring an extra kindness and harmony, to create the space in which the child is integrated, with openness to the community, and the parents to want the full development of the candidate for humanity. Contemporary pedagogy acknowledges that education at a very fragile age determines the harmonious development of the personality and a very good social integration.

The educator is called upon to use wisely the results of various types of progress to "train" individuals "as humanly" as possible, to know themselves and others, to love themselves and others, to cooperate and to harness the full creative potential for the development of society.

J. Delors identified the four pillars of education as "learning to know," "learning to do," "learning to live in communion with others" and "learning to be" (Delors, 2000). Assuming with all responsibility the role of "modelers" of the evolving human personality, even greater responsibility in the preschool age, when in training are all the psycho-physical and characteristic abilities of the children, the educators must aim to consolidate these four pillars of education. However, many times, the last of the pillars is neglected because of the desire to convey a lot of knowledge, to form many skills. Thus, we teach children "to know," "to do" and "to be," but we teach them less "how to live in communion with others." The affective needs of the child, extremely complex and numerous at the preschool age, the educational programs regarding the emotional development of the children, are analyzed superficially and not in their depth. Researches from the past decade have shown that difficulties in adapting to school life and the academic failure of children are due to insufficient emotional development while early emotional competence is closely linked to children's mental health, influences social interactions and relationships and ensures school success (Cassidy, 2000; Clipa, 2014a; European Commission, 2019; Ştefan & Kallay, 2010).

That is the reason for the importance given to these matters by the decisional structures of International and Romanian educational policies. These concerns led the National Education Ministry to organize in April 2014 the international conference entitled *Strengthening Early Childhood Education Systems: Investing Early to Ensure Effective Learning*, which focused on the emotional and psychosocial development of the preschool children. In September 2019, the European Commission published the comparative report about Data on Childhood Education and Care in Europe, and this document describes the main policy measures to ensure access specifying which countries guarantee a place in Early Childhood Education and Care from which age and it shows how investigation in this field has many benefits in entire life of these people. The papers highlighted the values of early age education and their effects on the children's social and emotional integration within that community (Clipa, 2014b; European Commission, 2019; A. Glava & C. Glava, 2002; Hart & Risley, 2013).The whole development process of the people is saturated and influenced by the socialization processes. An increasing number of researchers indicate that by helping children develop effective social and emotional skills, they will achieve very good, long-term results in health and well-being (Lantieri, 2017).

Chapter I

Development of social and emotional competences in early education

I.1 The development of affectivity in preschool

"Affectivity is a constant and necessary stimulus of any psychic development," says C. Bagdascar (1975), the center around which the other soul functions revolve even from the first days of our existence on earth. As energy, tendency, biological force, coexisting with the instincts of the ego, or as the will to live, it precedes intelligence. "Affective states determine the type of relationship established with the environment, determine the attitudes toward others and play an overwhelming role in the development of character and personality. Satisfaction or dissatisfaction of the affective need decisively influences the course of human life, the affectivity, by its fundamental character, mobilizing around it all the biopsychic energies of the person" (Bagdascar, 1975).

If we analyze the terms used by the *Psychology Dictionary*, coordinated by Ursula Şchiopu, the term has a more detailed explanation: "The attachment (engl. Attachment, fr. Attachement) is 'a complex intercommunication affective structure towards a person' (idea, ideology, group etc.)." The attachment comes with complex expression conduits (carelessness, protection, devotion and defense). The attachment toward small children was studied (Şchiopu, 1997; Verza & Verza, 2017), this issue being studied since the middle of last century. The study describes the affective reactions (imprinting phenomena) or its negative effects (hospitability phenomena). Attachment is focused on relationships between people and long-term relationship including parent and children. *A. Cosmovici* states that "there is awareness towards an accurate stimulus," analyzing the experiments of *K. Lorenz*, which proves that some animals, birds and even mammals have following and attachment reactions toward any bigger object that moves around them, from the first moments of life. Harlow's researches proved the "attachment" of a baby chimpanzee

toward a mother's "surrogate" by experiments. The baby chimp was isolated from his mother right after the birth, and put into the presence of
two metal skeletons, almost outlining the form of a monkey. One of them
was covered with soft cloth and the baby attached more to it although
the other one fed it. According to attachment theory, children internalize
the experiences of interactions with their primary tutors and formulate
mental representations of the caregivers during the second half of the first
year of their life. This affective links and representations are as a core-
value for entire life.

The attachment notion was introduced by *J. Bowlby* in 1969, bringing
an enormous contribution to the explanation of the mother-child relationship dynamics. Bowlby succeeds in elaborating an attachment theory. His
thesis recorded the following:

- The attachment need is the central element, and it is mandatory for the
  normal development of a toddler.
- The attachment is registered into the primary needs category, and
  according to Mallow's theory, there are elements of the attachment
  behavior even since birth (more or less premises of its development).

Bowlby's researches rouse interest for *Mary Ainsworth*, which succeeded
in classifying the attachment types developing a diagnosis methodology
of these types at very young ages (for her contribution to the development
of psychology is awarded in 1989 with the annual prize of Psychology
American Association). *Ainsworth* (1978) specifies that there is a fixed
and internal model of the attachment developed by the child toward a
person around him. The model distinguishes between strong and weak attachment. Within the weak attachment category, there are distinguished
three types: detached/fugitive, durable – ambivalent and perplexed/
unorganized.

The diagnosis of those three types of attachment is done by a lab technique developed by Ainsworth, called "unprecedented situation," and
"strange situation." The technique comprises eight episodes monitored
by the psychologist during which the baby is observed while he is in the
following rationalization situations:

- in his mother's presence;
- with his mother and a stranger;

- with a stranger;
- alone for a few minutes;
- with his mother again;
- alone again;
- with a stranger again;
- with a stranger and his mother.

Analyzing the results, the author defined the following types of attachment:

I.1.1 Strong/secure attachment

The child proves a certain degree (weak – moderate) of reaching closeness; he does not avoid the contact and does not resist to the steady contact with his mother; when he meets his mother again, he reacts positively; the mother can calm her child when he is upset. The choice for the mother, as opposed to the one for the stranger, is net.

I.1.2 Weak – fugitive/anxious attachment

The child avoids the contact with his mother especially when he meets her again after absence; he does not resist mother's closeness efforts, but he himself doesn't try to get into contact with her; the mother and stranger are treated the same.

I.1.3 Weak – durable attachment

The child is troubled when he is separated from the mother, who does not succeed to calm him down when she comes back. The child can avoid but also look for the contact depending on the moment; he can get angry with the mother when he meets her again, resisting to the stranger's efforts to get close to him.

I.1.4 Unorganized – weak attachment

The child seems blocked, disoriented, restless, being able to avoid contact and to look for it again; he is also able to have conflict behavior (e.g., he gets close to the mother but does not look at her) or to express affective states without any evident connection with the person concerned (mother/stranger).

These types of attachment could be noticed in different cultures, the most common type met being the strong attachment 60–65 %. Referring to these types of attachment, *Bowlby* (1980) says, "The children that have a stronger attachment with their mothers manifested separation anxiety, proving the attachment to the mother by the enthusiasm manifested toward her as a secure basis through which they can explore the world together". The anxious can be stronger attached to his mother, and she makes him happy, while the secure one perceives his mother as a "bonus." There are also children that are "stuck" to their mothers, afraid of the people and new partners, and do nothing to "explore the world" (Bowlby, 1980).

The researcher finds it useful dividing the attachment in secure, insecure and ambivalent.

Secure – the child can explore freely a strange situation using his mother as a secure basis, does not suffer a lot at the stranger's appearance and does not dramatize its mother's absence enjoying her coming back.

Insecure – the children that do not explore anything when mother is absent are very panicked by strangers, are desperate and disoriented but they do not seem to enjoy the return of the mother. In one of her presentations, *Ainsworth* considered that the particular secure signs can be proved by the children's reactions after a very short mother's absence. The secure children prove a very well organized sequential behavior: after mother's arrival and approaching, they want to be picked up and stay close to her. The presented answers of the insecure ones are either lack of interest or anger when she arrives.

The children assessed as secure within the experiment tend to be conscious and active at home as long as the mother is nearby; they cry only when they get hurt or the mother is very far. The adult is also available to the child's needs which he satisfies promptly. The children have a special relation with the teacher especially after they have spent a significant amount of time in kindergarten (Dirtu, 2016; Dumbrava, 2016; Golu, 2009). We can say that a good affective relation with their teacher will prepare them for adjusting easier to another school's affective and social style: the one of the elementary school teacher.

The children assessed as insecure within the experiment are inactive and agitated at home, even in the mother's presence, they cry suddenly and very often. This happens when the adult is not present enough for the affective needs of the child. At the kindergarten, these are the children that look for physical contact more often, are preoccupied by toys or any other activities, are inhibited when playing and are fearful and become anxious when separated (Golu, 2009). The adjustment to school is more difficult for these children, preschool children being in need for more information and training for this change.

Security – insecurity dimensions – in order to measure the child's attachment was of interest to many psychologists. Benedek, for example, talked about relations while Erickson described the basic trust during toddler period 0–1 years old. The child attachment quality is linked to the parental answer quality, a partnership that is permanently corrected in accordance with the answer.

Researchers detected that predictions can be done regarding the attachment type and that this is correlated to different personality aspects. The attachment variable was considered in most of the studies as having two values: secure attachment (strong) and insecure attachment (weak).

The attachment type correlated significantly with the following parameters:

I.1.4.1 Self-esteem and behavioral disorders

There is a strong correlation between the adult attachment type and the self-esteem decreased up to depression. Kobak, Cole, Ferenz-Gillies, Fleming and Gamble in 1993 suggest that depressive persons are usually the ones having an anxious-ambivalent attachment. All the researches emphasized the fact that all negative attachment models internalized are due to the conflict relations from toddler period. When in early life stress was identified, this is a major risk factor for emotional and behavioral issues for children and adults (Suzuki & Tomoda, 2015; Verza & Verza, 2017; Vrăsmaş, 1999). In a study (Lee & Hankin, 2009), it is showed that the relationship between anxious attachment and internalizing symptoms was mediated by dysfunctional attitudes and low self-esteem in adolescents. Low self-esteem and a high level of stress are predictors for the onset of depression. Numerous studies have explored the personality factors associated with social networking site addiction, with attachment style being a particularly significant predictor (Chen, 2019; Dirtu, 2016; Elias et al., 2007; Flynn, Liu & Ma, 2019; Noone & Sarma, 2018).

The children with a secure attachment style are not liable (in low percentages) to have behavioral disorders. In many of the analyzed studies, we've met these disorders at the avoidant attachment children as a result of the low self-esteem, hence the appearance of depressive moods and aggressiveness.

I.1.4.2 Sociability and addiction within social relations

There was noticed that those children strongly attached are more benevolent with children of the same age, and more appreciated by them, having many friends. They are also friendlier with adults they don't know, and are less afraid of them. Kim Crisholm did a very interesting study (Chisholm, 1998; Teodorescu, 1999) aiming at assessing both attachment and "non-discriminatory friendship" (toward any stranger). He did his study on a group of Romanian children (who lived for the last eight months at the orphanage) and two comparative groups: one of Canadian children who were never institutionalized, and a group of Romanian adopted children before being four months old.

The attachment was quantified by two measurements:

- Attachment questionnaire for the parents;
- Separation – reunion procedure for preschool children.

Non-discriminator friendship was studied by means of a questionnaire filled in by the parents (or tutor) that had to answer five questions regarding children behavior toward the adults. It resulted that the Romanian orphan children won with significantly different data than the Canadian ones. Between the adopted and orphan ones, there were no significant correlations regarding the relation toward the new strangers they met. A great difference was found when comparing the group of Romanian institutionalized children with the Canadian one, from the same perspective. The study concluded that those children with weak attachment have many behavior problems and also a low IQ score on Standfort-Binet scale.

In others studies (Clipa & Gavriluta, 2017; Elovainio et al., 2015; Hintsanen et al., 2009; Malouff, Thorsteinsson, & Schutte, 2005), shows high sociability is associated with strong attachment, building strong relationships, and favorable outcomes and low sociability with harmful outcomes (Richards & Hackett, 2012). Others researchers found associations between early childcare and the development of personality and social competence (Clipa & Schipor, 2015; Dumbrava, 2016; Gluschkoff et al., 2018; Osman et al., 2019; Verza & Verza, 2017); there is a lack of longitudinal studies on the possible effects of childcare arrangements on sociability in adulthood. Children with secure attachment find it easier to establish friendly relationships with peers, and they adapt better to the educational requirements in preschool and primary education (Verza & Verza, 2017).

An anxious attachment style is characterized by hyperactivity of the attachment system and the person is leading to a constant need to seek support and comfort. An avoidant attachment style leads to continual inhibition of psychological and social relationship needs, self-reliance and a marked distance from others (Chen, 2019; Flynn et al., 2019; Noone & Sarma, 2018). The research show that association between attachment and virtual sociability through social networking site (they obtain comfort and social support), prior studies found that attachment anxiety positively predicts, while avoidance negatively predicts, the addiction (Worsley, Mansfield & Corcoran, 2018).

I.1.4.3 Brotherhood relationships

The strongly attached children have better relations with their brothers and sisters, especially if they have a strong attachment too. The relations between them are considerably modified if the siblings prove a weak style of attachment (Stewart, 1983) or depends on the ages of children or parents strategies for managing siblings conflicts (Howe & Recchia, 2014).

I.1.4.4 Empathy

The securely attached children have emphatic abilities toward other adults or children. They feel the same as others and do not feel joy in others' pain. The low/avoidable attached children present that behavior described above.

Understanding others' feelings is based on knowing your own emotions and feelings. The children are able to understand feelings since 3 years old, helped by an adult, and beginning with the age of 5–6 years old, they are able to identify it with a minimum help from parents. In this period, children with secure attachment express more empathy than others, and they are more sociable and positively perceive their peers (Elias, Tobias & Friendlander, 2007; Ştefan & Kallay, 2010). The empathy helps children to understand other persons and to use a more appropriate strategy for emotional regulation.

In the article "Attachment Security and Child's Empathy: The Mediating Role of Emotion Regulation" is underline the multiple factors who are influenced different levels of empathy as: attachment, negative emotionality, and emotion regulation (Panfile & Deborah, 2012).

I.1.4.5 Collaborative manner

High scores regarding the collaborative manner were given to the secure children without being however considered "obedient." They are easier to discipline and self-discipline without the permanent intervention from adults (Clipa & Schipor, 2015; Lopez et al., 1997).

In this aspect is very important one of factor as affective communication which is a way through the children express and receive feelings and is necessary for building team working (Verza & Verza, 2017) and for develop entire personality of the preschools.

I.1.4.6 Problem-solving and creativity

The secure attachment children have a better ability to focus on the free games activity, without requiring a theme. They approach the entire problem situations with confidence and are able to use "the world of objects." They find effective solutions to use when adjusting them to the right situation, and they can add innovation in educational process (Kirrane et al., 2019).

In numerous studies, either strong correlations with other personality structures (Chisholm, 1998) or the style's time sustainability has been analyzed (Carlson, 1998). They proved that the type of attachment formed between the ages of 1 and 3 (around eighteen months old) becomes permanent in similar living conditions (Lopez et al., 1997). It becomes an intern role model according to which it will react and behave as an adult.

Within a study done on a forty-six children plot (26 between the ages of 4 and 5 years old and 20 between 6 and 7 years old), we proved that there are roles almost identical in time; for example, the leaders are the ones rejected by many of them. In order to measure the children's degree of sociability, I tried to adjust these techniques to preschool age. I took pictures in the same frame to each child and then I put on a table all the pictures of the children from the group and two baskets: a black and a red one. Each child's task was to choose the pictures of their playmates and of those that do not want in the group. The total number of votes (positive and negative) led to an acceptance or rejection index calculus within the group. The ones who were elected a lot are the children with leadership abilities while the rejected ones are the avoided, not the accepted. In order to check time sustainability of the results, I repeated the method again after 6–7 months. I designed an alternative for those of 4–5 years old under the form of a train with a locomotive and two wagons: a crimson one and a dark blue one. Each wagon had cut seats in order to place their classmates' pictures in. Their task was to choose whom they want to go on the trip with and whom not (the red wagon leaves on the trip and the blue one does not). One of the conclusions was that the roles with many choices were the same, fact that proves that preschoolers have rather constant criteria in choosing their favorite classmates. There might be certain fixed structures at a small age, which become internalized and a characteristic type to each personality.

Another conclusion of the research was the one that preschool children at 4–5 years old do many more choices than the 6–7 years old ones (the difference between averages 9,46 against 6,05, and $p < 0,001$), though the contemporary theories assert that at the ages of 4–5 years old, the children are in a conflict phase. It could be that the middle group children are not very well bounded, having the tendency to choose almost all the classmates. Another explanation would be that the middle group preschool desires to gain on his part the potential playmates. The number of rejections is higher at the preparatory class group (6–7 years old). The average difference is 1,8 (5,65 against 3,849), and $p = 0,22$. A possible explanation would be that the grown up ones have already spent more years together forming more solid hierarchy criteria, but they are more mature cognitively and affectively. Thus, the socialization happens according to sensitivity emphasis toward one another and with the development of the ability to see beyond the egocentrism and even accepting others' influences. This is all about "a co-building" (Booth, Rubin, & Krasmer, 1998; Ciofu, 1998; Clipa, 2014a; Iacob, 1999; Petrovai et al., 2012; Petrovai & Petrica, 2013), which supposes both relation competences symmetry as well as a common aim, which will make the partners combine their efforts and knowledge to fulfill their aim. This common effort can evolve either into a socio-cognitive conflict or to cooperation, both being reduced into the general micro-social relations.

At the preschool age, the manifestations of "holotypic" affectivity are the vital affective manifestations, especially the emotions. The preschool child possesses a very wide range of emotions, whose nuances are continually deepening the life in the community, causing a continuous complication of the affective reactions toward the others. Thus, the affective reactions are not only amplified quantitatively but also enriched qualitatively with new forms of expression. Through imitation, the child takes on a series of affective states, along with the emotional expressions that accompany them, and his emotional behaviors diversifying and acquiring a much greater degree of coherence, adaptability. In the recent research, Rizzolatti and Craighero (2004) discover a group of neurons called mirror neurons, which are on the front of the brain, in the frontal lobes, and they explain how and why the children read/understand feeling and cognition of other people and develop empathy for them. This explains the complexity of imitation process which is fundamental for entire development from motor skills to emotional competences (Dumbrava, 2016).

At the same time, the capacity to simulate affective states in order to satisfy the different needs is increased. The clash between the extremely numerous temptations at this age and the restrictions imposed by the adult regarding their satisfaction, between the child's desire to satisfy the adult he loves and the moral rules imposed by the latter, generate an extremely wide spectrum of emotional experiences. Thus appears the pride, modesty and the "prestige crises" in public reprimand, as well as the "bitter candy" syndrome, which describes an emotional state of shame, lived by the child around the age of 6, after receiving an unmerited reward, the joy cause by the reward being overshadowed by the anxiety born of a critical attitude toward one's own behavior.

Also at preschool age, the foundation of the ego is laid, the child being able to detach from others as a self-contained entity, being aware that he is "someone" compared to his other colleagues. Considering the unifying function of affectivity, presented above, it can be said that the unity of the ego is the direct expression of the functioning of the affectivity, and the affective life at infant age is the basis of the future personality of the child. More important than instruction itself, because it precedes and conditions it, affectivity is the primal food of the soul life, shaping the organic constitution that is about to be reached by the child. The evolutionary curve of the individual biography is conditioned by the emotional atmosphere of childhood.

The essential function of the affective processes as well as their expressions is to put the body in agreement with the situation, to adapt, permanently regulating the human behavior. The affectivity is thus integrated into the general mechanism of the adaptation of the organism, in the general function of regulating the behavior, the initial disorganization caused by strong emotions, leading finally to a higher organization. If the sensory processes provide us with information on the surrounding reality, on the nature of the objects, "the meaning of the stimulus," the affective processes inform us on their value, on their usefulness for the good state of the subject and on the "sense of the stimulus," the significance and meaning together constituting the "meaning" of the objects, phenomena and situations of the surrounding reality.

M. Roco believes that emotions are what ensure survival (emotions, as an internal guidance system, delicate and sophisticated, which alert us when we lack natural impulse), decision-making (emotions, as a valuable source of information), setting boundaries in order to protect our mental and psychic health, communication with others (through emotional expressions) and, last but not least, unity with other members of the society (feelings unite us, convictions separate us – Rocco, 2000).

V. Pavelcu and Verza reveal the unifying function of affectivity by the fact that "any intellectual or motor process is enveloped in feeling" and "logical unification and rational synthesis precede a syncretic, affective unification" (Verza & Verza, 2017). The affectivity thus appears to us, not as a component in the internal structure of the psychic life, but as a "symbiosis" with the other components, as a binder of all the psychic components, a factor that confers the full meaning of the psychic life. The development of some components of the psychic life depends on this binder, the unifying function of the affectivity affecting the whole human activity, on all the psychic processes, either in the sense of the expected progress, or in the sense of the unwanted regress. The very functioning of the self as a whole is influenced by this unifying function of affectivity, considered by some psychologists to be the "core," the germs of personality, most of the possible behavioral disorders of children having their origin in the affective binder. "The whole development of the personality is dominated by the search for a certain coherence, of an organization of values that excludes the internal tears (or that seeks them only to extract new systematic perspectives from them)" (Piaget & Inhelder, 1969).

I.2 Social and emotional competence in the preschool period

Regarding the factors that are part of the adjustment and life success, processes of great importance were the factors that deal with emotions (Alison & James, 2008; European Commission, 2019; Ștefan & Kallay, 2010). The process, per se, has an ontogenetic evolution, which is submitted to the general socio-historic evolution by means of numerous contents transmitted from generation to generation, as a social competence. The socialization process is a concept that is used to describe and explain how the future "candidates to humanity" adopt behavior necessary to their adjustment to the culture and society they belong to. "It is the process by which a person acquires the rules of conduct, beliefs and attitudes of a society or a social group, so that it could function within" (Malim, Birch & Hayward, 2000; Champbell, 2001).The author emphasizes the determinative and formative role of the existent affective relationships between the persons within the social group. If there are positive inter-relations, we assign a person the ability of being *sociable*. This is the characteristic that expresses the feature of a human being to look for contacts and social relationships, to engage gladly in initiating and maintaining communication of any type. According to the efficiency and facility with which the relationships are maintained, one can diagnose the *social intelligence* (as a matter of multiple intelligences which could target more aspects of personality adjustment).

In literature we find the term *social competence* (Bisquerra, 2007; Clipa, 2014; Ignat, 2011; Goleman, 2007; Verza & Verza, 2017), which expresses the manifestation of adequate and adjusted behaviors from a social point of view, which has positive consequences on the person involved and allows reaching certain targets. Social competence is defined as the ability to handle social interactions effectively. In other words, social competence refers to getting along well with others, being able to form and maintain close relationships, and responding in adaptive ways in social settings (Weiner & Craighead, 2010). Given the complexity of social interaction, this competence is a result of cognitive abilities, emotional skills and processes, social awareness and personal and professional values regarding interpersonal relationships. Social competence is influencing emotional competence whose ability is to understand emotions and to has an appropriate behavior.

The socio emotional competence for preschool children are quantified by the ability of the children to initiate social relationships with adults and other children (Carlson, 1998; Petrovai et al., 2012). These abilities are divided into two categories: interpersonal and intrapersonal abilities (Petrovai et al., 2012; Ştefan & Kallay, 2010). The development of the social competences is present within the new European and Romanian curricula by introducing the curricula regarding the creation of a positive psychological environment and by the educational reform for the well-being in the kindergarten environment as a key competence. It is necessary that the *socialization* process is done full and complete.

As *U. Şchiopu* (1997) asserts, "socialization is the continuous process (unequal in intensity) by which certain role models for values and behavior forms are understood, assessed and identified within the groups they belong to, and their acceptance as belonging there" (Şchiopu, 1997). It is for sure "that the socio-affective development is in close interrelation with the self-consciousness shaping process, as well as with the intellectual and moral development parameters" (A. Glava & C. Glava, 2002). The influences are exerted even before birth, continuing then with the large family-environment relationship, as well as the interactions between people of the same age. *B.F. Skinner* considered that it can be taken into account a primary, elementary sociability, which could be formed since the first years of life, but remaining the base for the whole ulterior evolution. As the same author asserts, there is a secondary sociability, more complex and refined, linked to the intricate adjustment to the multiple environment aspects (the social laws and values have a role of "adjustment" for the way to be). At the beginning, the social relations are reduced to mother–child and child–family interactions. The sociability begins by means of the social smile, namely the reaction toward any person. Next, it becomes selective, reacting with anxiety and crying toward strangers. After the first year of life, the toddler's social universe is enlarged. Because of the linguistic and motor skills, it succeeds to communicate both with the adults and other children. The adjustment process will take place in concentric circles by the enlarged use of needs, attitudes and base conducts. Some authors assert that by the age of three the human being acknowledges 60 % of the fundamental experience. In preschool, the environments in which socializing is done are diversified and multiplied, the preschool children getting into contact with the kindergarten and the enlarged family and social environments (street, transportation means, museums, parks, etc.).

Although integrated into the same life, these three environment components require to the child not only behavioral adjustments to systems of requirements slightly different, in different conditions of tutoring, protection and affection, but also a great sense of world and life diversity, a more dense and complex training of decisions, curiosity, emotions and knowledge in new situations. These are the conditions of child's personality development, its ability to communicate and project in the context of his life events. The psychical processes are evolving: the perception and representations are enriched, creativity acquires higher values, emotions are fully manifested and the symbolism is more and more complex. All these give uniqueness and entitle this period of life "childhood's golden age" (Şchiopu, 1997).

The child is impressed by the social interactions surrounding it. Mead claims that the elements surrounding him stimulate his personality differently. All the people around the child work as "mirror-egos" that define him, and while the sense of continuity and identity evolves, he does not separate from the roles he plays, namely to react proportionally to the adults' image about them. Mead asserts that the Ego, under all its aspects, is a social product. The relationships with the persons less close to the child are actually attempts, conditioned according to their type of personality. The social relationship takes place enriching the communication ways by language forms (verbal or nonverbal) and filtering out these feelings by moral values. Emotions are mediated by analyzing the situation through the moral values as a superior level of moral socializing (A. Glava & C. Glava, 2002; Vrăşmaş, 2014). Every acquirement of the child is a stage in his emotional maturation and in defining his emotional and social intelligence. Another psychologist, Vîgotski, notices that permanent socialization is a continuous confrontation of the child with its social environment in which he learns the language and communication types, modeling its own thoughts and ideas. He introduced the "social development situation" concept, including in its spheres the conjugated effects of the external and internal agents. That situation is typical for each stage, defining the dynamics and the abilities specific to each maturation stage.

Wallon estimates that the interpersonal relations between 3 and 6 years are more important than the ones fixed around the age of 7–12 years, because the child tends to a progressive autonomy (Wallon, 1978). *Erikson,* another researcher, notices that the autonomy might happen around the ages of 2 or 3. He classifies this evolution into three stages: 0–1 years – trust is dominant, 2–3 years old – autonomy and 4–5 years old – initiative. These stages describe the relationships with the others, both adults they imitate as well as other children of different ages. The adult behavior is thoroughly transposed in playing situations, in which diverse status-roles are seriously acted.

According to the *theory of socio-emotional development* described by E. Erikson (1968, 2015), resolving the conflicts that arise between the child's possibilities of relationship and the demands of the social environment determines new psychosocial acquisitions. Of the eight development stages described by the author, the preschooler is in the third, experiencing the conflict between initiative and guilt, successfully overcoming the conflict by encouraging his/her creativity and curiosity, generating a positive future attitude toward study, interrelation and work.

Knowing as deeply as possible the affective life of the children, through a continuous and increased attention, in the context of the game and of the compulsory activities, but also systematically through different methods and procedures, determines a better understanding of their behavioral expressions. The essence of the educative-educational activity of the educator in the kindergarten lies precisely in the focus on the affective life of the children and on his/her functioning mechanisms. Satisfaction of the affiliation needs of the children that determines the affective transfer and affective identification, the triggering of a scenic affective climate in all the actions taken, the use of didactic strategies accompanied by the corresponding affective load are all premises of the continuity or, sometimes, of the substitution of the family's affective climate, to shelter the child from any possible emotional frustrations, which can have negative consequences on the harmonious development of his personality. All this is not only a challenge, but also a duty for the educator, a barometer of appreciation of his/her work, whose fruits will not be picked up immediately, but in time, sometimes throughout the entire human development. "Children need love and understanding. Let's let children have their childhood, and the kindergarten will remain in their soul as a dear place, and for us the gratitude that we have done everything to be the dearest and most wonderful place, that we have loved them very much, we have protected them with affection and we have respected them" (M. Debesse, 1981).

The beginning of preschooling determines the diversification and enrichment of the affective states, since the efforts to adapt to the new social requirements, to the enlarged social environment, must be amplified. The unprecedented, new and diverse social situations in which the child is involved often cause anxiety and nervousness. One can observe an instability of the emotional experiences, emotional outbursts, a sudden transition from a positive to a negative state and vice versa. The need for autonomy of the child who discovers his/her self collides with the prohibitions imposed by the adult, giving rise to different emotional experiences that take the form of the crisis of opposition manifested by rivalry made by adults in the most unexpected forms. The transition to moral feelings such as shame (when violating the norms of conduct), contentment (when appreciated), attachment and love to the brothers and friendship (the preference to play with certain children) is reinforced.

In the middle school, the emotional reactions are more controlled and more in accordance with the demands imposed by the educator or the group of children, the behaviors are more nuanced, being under the sign of the daily rules of the family and kindergarten. Affective experiences are still related to the present circumstances, "here" and "now," still having a dominant situational character. The middle schooler lives the moment intensely, is little influenced by stringent obligations and needs, is anchored at present and everything that gains significance and relief in a concrete context determines and motivates his emotional experiences. The renunciation of some of his passing desires, the manifestation of resistance to frustration and postponement, denotes a beginning of the organization of the will.

Based on the background of a good family environment, the preschooler begins to present acute moments of opposition to the adult, the demands that are manifested towards him, opposition followed, most of the times, by wishes for reconciliation. He learns to appreciate the behavior of those around him, to know, in part, the social value of human actions, learning through active and passive imitation numerous ways to react, belonging to the family or the group of children he comes in contact with, easily adapting not only in the kindergarten environment, but also in contact with any kind of new situation. The active requirement of being useful to those around (especially adults) is now being established.

Grown-ups behavior is precisely transposed in role-playing, where different status-roles are seriously acted. Thus one can notice that the favorite theme of the role-playing games chosen imitates social relations. Socialization is done efficiently with children of the same age too. Children pass through various stages along their sociological evolution. First stage could be the solitary activity, during the first years of life, when no attention is given to children of the same age, and tends to treat them as objects, "social relations" reducing frequently everything to the effort of mastering a desired object. The last stage reveals the group activity organization (6–7 years). The stages of transition are the ones during which the others are framed as playing partners, more and more needful, the individual passing from "each one for his own" and spectator of the others' activity attitude, to active social interactions, though sporadic and limited at first. This evolution is explainable since the vocabulary is amazingly enriched, assuring a more safe and efficient communication. Osterieth, analyzing the game types, indicates the presence of "the parallel and isolated or associative game," at the age of two or three (Osterrieth, 1976).

This is the stage where children look for each other and are glad to spend time together in groups of two or three, each one of them being very sensitive at the others presence, but paying attention to their individual activity. Communication attempts are rare and less successful, so that one cannot speak about a group activity organization. From five years old, the author entitles calls the game as being associative; the group is enlarged to four or five partners, with more frequent and longer interactions; they make deals, conventions and regulations of the activity that has as many attempts as that of a collective organization. These are always threatened by a tendency to egocentrism of each partner, and everyone's lack of ability to have group representation of their common objective. The limits between game types are not established for good at the above-mentioned age. Within the nowadays egocentrism, the child is perceived as a threat; he does nothing but interfering others' activity and disturb their developing projects. That's why the conflicts and fights are usual, but short. Their frequency tends to drop with the age and increase in duration. The child asks the nearest adult for help and thus the "denunciation" situation is revealed both within the institutional environment, as well as in society.

Various specialists proved that boys talk more than girls, and to the usual partners more than to the occasional ones. *Zazzo* notices that girls cooperate better while boys are more isolated. During pair work activities, it was observed that when the children are smaller than 4 years old, they can be fascinated by the partners' game. The child does not aim at imitating the other or having its toy, but spending time with the other one. There are many circumstances in which children fight during visits. Giving them a toy similar to the one they want does not solve the problem. Cousinet asserted that the "free understanding" from the playgrounds would be the basis of social life, and in the same time the effect of normal social development at a certain status. In his book *Social Life and Group Activity* he establishes the following stages in child socialization: the individual stage (2–5 years old) and the first social life stage (5–6 years old) materialized in rule games where the child feels the need of comparing himself with the others.

Greenberg's researches proved that the competitive and imitative spirits are intensified at this age. One can notice that at the age of three, 42,6 % of the children have a similar behavior, the percentage increasing at the age of four to 69,2 %, 75 % at the age of five and 86,5 % at seven years old. The frequency of friendships increases to preschool children, meaning that social integration tendencies are spontaneously displayed. It is considered that the interpersonal relations in this stage are established according to the moment, and are influenced by affectivity. "The group life is marked by syncretic sociability, generating liability of the relations in a very dense field" (Vrăşmaş, 2014). All these socialization processes are mediated by the attachment type formed in early childhood and by its general affective development. During preschool, the child lives intensely affective, but he also has developed the possibility of comparison and refinement of the affective conduits so that the impulses linked to affectivity are acknowledged. The attachment and the numerous components and actions are approached in various magazines and specialty books. Although affectivity evolution is difficult to quantify, empirically approach the complex matter of the personality affective "block" trying to capture the quantitative and qualitative character of the phenomena. The authors of the studies try to prove that the attachment formed between the ages of 1 and 3 (around 18 months old) becomes permanent in seemingly life conditions for that person. It will become an internalized model according to which the person will react his whole life and form a social adjustment style.

The child can adapt to the environment through behavior, depending on the emotion he lives, the emotions and behavioral reactions being closely correlated. However, if the adult, parent or educator does not teach the child to pay attention to his or her emotions, the adaptation to his needs may become deficient; the child learning that what he feels is not good leads to the formation of negative beliefs about himself. "The child learns from the relationship with the adult to be attentive to their feelings, to recognize their emotions and to understand what each of them transmits, in order to adapt to their needs" (Petrovai et al., 2012).

The ability to control how we react to emotions is not an innate trait. From the first month of the child's life, it is the parent who observes the child's emotions and helps him to change his behavior, in order to be able to adapt to the circumstances. Often, the strong emotions experienced by the child, of frustration or anger, reflect nothing more than too great differences between his needs and his behavioral resources, for example the need for reward and the behavioral resources necessary to obtain the reward. In order to develop the essential competences in the development of the child's self-control, the adult, parent or educator intervenes in such situations, helping the child to adapt to the situation, facilitating his access to the reward, or, conversely, teaching him to delay the reward and tolerance to frustration. The older the child grows, the more his or her emotional autonomy and emotion management capacity must increase, as he or she learns from adults how to manage them, such as changing perspectives or changing behavior. "Emotional development is influenced by the quality of the children's relationship with parents and educators. When the educator observes and pays attention to the child's emotions, he sends the message to the child that they are healthy and that they are an important source of adaptation to the environment. The way parents and educators respond when the child experiences an emotion shapes his or her attitude toward emotions. When the educator and the parent express emotions and manage their emotions soundly, the child learns how to respond to emotions' (Petrovai et al., 2012).

The role of emotions in the child's life is overwhelming as long as he is supported to discover his own emotions and those of others and to find ways of "healthy" reaction to his own emotions. Petrovai et al. (2012) identifies several ways in which the educator can support the child in this regard, namely:

– accepts and notices the child's emotions;
– identifies and offers a safe environment for expressing emotions, without punishing by ridiculing, criticizing, denying or minimizing their expression;
– familiarizes children with the expression of emotions by initiating and encouraging mime-type dramatizations or games in which the characters express different emotions;
– helps children understand their own emotions by discussing the characters in the stories, how they think or feel;
– encourages children to respond to emotions through healthy behaviors, rewarding them every time this occurs;
– supports children in differentiating between their own emotion and the other's emotion as a result of his behavior, without punishing or blaming the child;

– permanently helps children differentiate behavioral emotion, for example, anger, from inappropriate behavior such as hitting a colleague.

The child begins to act inappropriately, often displaying problematic behaviors that neither he nor the adult can handle properly, when he is not supported and does not learn to pay attention to his emotions, which are his main source of adaptation. By not paying attention to the emotional needs of the child, the adult often punishes the child's behavior and, because he is not aware of the emotion and the need for adaptation, the child learns to mentally associate a certain situation with an emotion he had previously experienced, displaying inappropriate behavior in a similar situation just because he anticipates that he will feel the same.

"The child learns what emotions are and how to react to them, observing the behavior of the adult" (Petrovai et al., 2012). The responsibility for the emotional development of the children lies with adults, parents and educators. D. Petrovai identifies three mistakes that they frequently make in the relationship with the child and which impede their emotional development and can lead to the formation of negative beliefs about the child (it is not good what I feel, I do not deserve to be appreciated and I am not worthy of the love of others, etc.) and to a poor adaptation to the needs he feels. These are:

– blaming the child for his own emotions;
– verbal and nonverbal expression, in the presence of children, of their own emotions without taking into account the fact that he, as an educator must possess emotional autonomy, which implies the ability to manage emotions without harming others;
– punishment of the child's expression of emotions, which inevitably leads to their attempt to suppress them, to ignore them and "ignoring does not make the emotion disappear, but rather amplifies it," degenerating into maladaptive behaviors difficult to manage.

The adaptive role of children's emotions is an aspect that educators should not overlook in carrying out the daily instructional-educational process, "the emotions being those that teach us what are the emotional needs without which we cannot live in balance with ourselves. Ignoring these signals in our brain is like ignoring hunger or thirst. Sooner or later there would be an imbalance" (Petrovai et al., 2012; Petrovai & Petrica, 2013). This is why it is imperative that "the academic education of the children is coherently supported by a social-emotional one, which will allow them a better adaptation to the complexity of daily life" (Opre, 2010).

Children's emotional health is influenced by their growing ability to express, understand and regulate different emotions. Emotional competence was defined as having three specific components: emotional expressivity, emotional knowledge and emotional regulation (Denham et al., 2003). Each of these plays a key role in determining the ability of young children to interact and form relationships with other people. This affective communication is very important for growing up the level of general intelligence and emotional intelligence (Verza & Verza, 2017).

Emotional expressiveness, the ability to express different emotions, is a basic component of emotional competence. Models of positive expression of emotions, such as happiness, are helpful in developing friendly relationships, while negative expressions of emotions, such as anger, interfere with peer relationships. Children often develop characteristic emotional responses, and these patterns of expressiveness either lead to positive interactions with peers of the same age, or become barriers to successful interactions. The relationships with equals are a factor of development and affective progress, which diminishes the child's self-centeredness, maintained by the family, with or without permission. The presence of children of the same age with him, to whom the educator relates in the same way, makes the child not only discover himself, but also to discover the others, to consider not only his experiences, but also the experiences of those of same age, which resemble him and are yet so different. Interacting daily with his peers, recognizing in them the same needs and possibilities as himself, the child, tactfully led by the educator, gradually develops long-lasting altruistic behaviors, develops empathy, recognizing more easily the emotional states of the others and better modulating their communication and collaboration acts with them.

Emotional knowledge involves identifying and labeling one's own emotions as well as the emotional expressions of others and the appropriate response to the displayed emotional expressions. Children who understand the expressions or the emotions of others usually associated with social situations are more able to respond in a prosocial manner and are considered to be fonder of colleagues and teachers. The ability to recognize emotional expressions is a foundation for the further acquisition of additional information about emotions, such as the causes and consequences of emotions, their most subtle manifestations, social rules on emotions and emotional labels used in the language to which the child is exposed. For example, the child sees a person in a certain situation and then relies on the facial expressions of the person to determine what emotion the situation caused. Thus, emotional understanding is added to the understanding of emotions, as a basic component of emotional competence. Educators influence children's knowledge of emotions by discussing emotions during daily interactions. Assimilation of words related to emotions takes place through deliberate teaching, children being directed to label both negative and positive emotions, as well as to understand the causes of these emotions and healthy ways of expressing them.

Emotional regulation, also an important element of emotional competence, implies the ability to manage emotion and behavior during social interaction. Young children have limited resources for emotional regulation, and emotions – both positive and negative – can overwhelm the child, which often leads to disorganized thinking and problematic behavior (Ashiabi, 2000). Children who have difficulty in emotional regulation often present emotional expressions that appear aggressive or intense. This interferes with the ability of these children to interact with others in a socially acceptable manner. Both children and adults are likely to have negative perceptions of such emotional responses. Cultivating and individualizing the educator-child relationships offer important contexts for promoting the emotional health of the children. As they interact with children, educators have the opportunity to prepare children for appropriate responses during peer interactions and classroom activities, while also serving as models of appropriate expression of emotions.

Research suggests that a child's emotional development status has an impact in all areas of child development. Development in the physical, social, cognitive and emotional fields all contribute to a child's ability to adapt to school life. It has been shown that especially emotional competence is deeply linked to social competence.

Social, emotional, and cognitive learning are interconnected to a greater extent in younger children. Therefore, building emotional skills assists children in forming positive social relationships and positive self-esteem and is essential for ongoing school preparation and academic success.

Beyond the family environment and the interactions with parents and carers, the context of the kindergarten group offers unlimited opportunities to promote emotional health and competence. Each encounter with a child provides an opportunity to support the development of emotional skills, which will allow children to experience success in the classroom and in other contexts. Throughout the day, children are involved in a variety of routine, planned and spontaneous activities. By participating in the dynamic of the group, children experience, and at the same time express a variety of emotions – some in ways that suggest a positive course of development and others that may indicate harmful effects on a child over time.

Educators play an important role in promoting healthy development by identifying behaviors that may interfere with healthy emotional response patterns (Ashiabi, 2000). However, educators are rarely trained in the assessment and promotion of emotional competence. This lack of training often causes educators to minimize or overlook the implications of emotional competence, and the dysfunctions that arise in the emotional development of preschool children are a precursor to behavioral problems in early and middle childhood.

Early emotional competence – which includes emotional regulation, expression and emotional knowledge – is closely linked to children's mental health, and it influences their social interactions and relationships, and affects school success. Teachers play a crucial role in promoting emotional skills by forming and cultivating specific, individualized relationships with children, modeling children's emotional responses during social interactions and during activities and routines, by providing a healthy emotional expression model, by developing understanding emotions and creating environments in which children feel appreciated and can thrive. Careful observation of children in different contexts in the classroom allows educators to perform an analysis of current levels of emotional competence and a plan to promote mental health. Such efforts are essential to ensure the development of the skills necessary for children to function effectively in a range of social and school contexts.

Chapter II

Early childhood education through outdoor activities – theoretical frame

Early childhood education is a priority of Romanian and European education and a means of increasing the quality of the European life. This is an important aspect for the development of the society and of any community that wants to adapt to current and future trends. In contemporary writings, we find that educational intervention at the early age determines the harmonious personality construction and a very good social insertion (Clipa, 2014). Concerns about this topic have led the Ministry of National Education to organize the international conference *Strenghtening Early Childhood Education Systems: Early Investing to Ensure Effective Learning* in 2014, focusing on the psychosocial and emotional development of children since early ages. Within the papers presented, the values of the early educational interventions and their effects on the social and emotional integration of the children in the respective community were emphasized (Hart & Risley, 2013).

In order to understand the topic of this study, it is necessary to present the theoretical perspectives on children and childhood, to analyze the main theories in order to notice how they have influenced and still influence the lives of children. The theories referred to here examine the child and childhood from many points of view, such as the psychology of development, philosophy and sociology with which they have many things in common, and which effectively contribute to an interdisciplinary understanding of childhood. Talcott Parsons' theory of social action, along with Jean Piaget's Theory of Cognitive Development had a tremendous impact on raising and educating children in most parts of the world. These are, in turn, built on the philosophical ideas of the period of Enlightenment, "childhood is not at all known: and with our misconceptions, as we advance, we will be wandering. The wisest writers refer to what matters for people to know, regardless of whether the child is capable of learning.

They always look at the adult in the child, without thinking about what the child is, before becoming an adult" (Jenks, 2005). Understanding childhood requires clarifying the positioning of childhood in relation to maturity and the interaction between the child and the adult. In these theories, the child was regarded as vulnerable, immature and unexperienced, who is to become a rational and responsible adult with a high morality. "The new childhood sociology has firmly argued that there is no need for a specific set of methods to investigate the lives of children. Sociologists are critical of the trend of the developmental psychology of seeing the child as an immature adult and a developing person, rather than a competent and complete social actor" (Greene & Hogan, 2005).

Talcott Parsons (1902–1979) developed the theory of socialization in which a hierarchical system of norms, values and a social structure are implemented from top to bottom in the society. The system would ensure harmony and balance in the society; each person should find its place and role, as if they were wheels in a mechanism that would work smoothly. The underlying themes of developmental psychology are closely linked to the values of a natural, universal, foolish and immature child, and this has argued for the sociological explanation of childhood in the form of socialization theories. Sociologists believe that what is important in order to become an adult is not our biological nature, but the learning process by which the society teaches children the norms and values that are important to maintain social order. "The shift from one state to another is accomplished according to the theory of socialization through the natural process of development (from simple to complex, from irrational to rational) and through the equally natural process of being a parent" (Richards & Taylor, 1998). The theory has been seen as a universal model with no room for cultural differences or historical time. In reality, people play specific roles and the outlook on the child is not relevant; he or she has to adapt to the behavioral patterns set by adults in order to perform certain functions.

Jean Piaget (1896–1980) was concerned about the cognitive development of children, being known for his contributions to developmental psychology, and laid the foundations for the cognitive development theory. Childhood psychology is a specialized branch of traditional psychology focusing on children, mainly the study of children's psychological processes and, in particular, how these processes differ from adults. Psychologists are interested in how certain behaviors develop, how the influence of the environment on the development of the child develops to some extent. Piaget saw the child as having the potential to develop at different stages, from the stage of sensory-motor development to the ultimate goal, of reaching an obvious social and intellectual maturity (Piaget, 1976). The child's development will take place through the assimilation process, when a new experience will be compared and added to the existing scheme in the child, and this would lead to a change and refinement, the child being at another stage of development. A schema is a structure of the child's internal actions. "From this perspective, developmental psychology can be seen as a discourse that contributes not only to building our children's images and understanding children's needs, but also to building and creating the entire landscape of childhood" (Dahlberg, Moss & Pence 1999).

Piaget describes the issue of child development as a product of heritage or environment. Etymologically, the word heritage comes from the Latin term "patrimonium" which has the following meaning: "what is inherited from the father." Heritage, therefore, contains a double dimension, on the one hand belonging to a community, on the other hand transmitting an inheritance. The dominant principle in Piaget's theory is that knowledge is not transferred from one person to another, but is built by each individual based on the experience he has gradually accumulated. He believed that humans are not robots that respond automatically to a learning situation. It is the child who builds his own knowledge, and for this reason, the child's knowledge is acquired through learning and experience. Explicitly, Piaget, who was a biologist, considered that due to the materiality of the biological basis, the child's development is universal. His theories saw children and childhood as a standard for measuring normality in terms of the child's intellectual development (Piaget, 1976).

For both theories, the hypothesis was developed from a natural and universal perspective. The child has been researched as a universal concept, and the natural can be biologically explained, everything is found in the child. The idea of linear progress and universalist development is the foundation of these theories; the child, no matter where he lives or in what era he finds himself, can be qualitatively appreciated.

Modern theories regarding cognitive development have as their main objective the "renegotiation" of the relationship between education and human intelligence. In fact, most of the theories regarding "intelligence," using only Piaget's activity, refer to the human potential to learn and acquire an ability, independent of cultural values and contingent situations. Different cultures favor and therefore promote different types of intelligence depending on the functionality they have in the context of everyday life. Thus, Howard Gardner, a contemporary American scholar who teaches at Harvard University, articulates the human cognitive device on seven distinct types of intelligence: verbal-linguistics, logic-mathematics, spatial, kinesthetic, musical, intrapersonal and interpersonal. Recently, he proposed the addition of two more, the naturalistic and the philosophical-existential one. "Culture is, therefore, the interpretive key of the methods and directions of development of intelligence. Another merit of Gardner is that he highlighted how, from birth, children from every culture learn to master symbolic systems and develop a whole series of intuitive knowledge" (DeCanale, 2016).

The modern point of view of childhood originates from two great philosophers of Enlightenment era, John Locke and Jean Jacques Rousseau. They still influence today our conception on child and childhood. It describes the concept of "wild" child. "In many respects, this theory is a resumption of social thinking of the nineteenth century. Just as the evolutionary anthropologist, self-titled civilized person, simply knew that the savage differs from itself on an evolutionary scale and therefore deserves to be studied, so are we, as rational adults, perceive the child as different, less developed and being in need of answers"(Jenks, 2005).

The educational system of the last centuries has been built on the basis of original sin, designing a child naturally affected by bad instincts. In the religious life, man must strive for his salvation by living an honest life in fear of God. This includes self-discipline, personal sacrifices to resist bodily and worldly temptations, to have a compassionate life. The children were seen as ignorant and sinful. Parents had to make sure that they follow the teachings, or discipline and constrain their anarchic impulses in order to ensure their salvation, and education was needed everywhere. Children's lives have changed from a relative freedom to the strict conditions at home or at school, where they spent more time away from their parents. Today's constant monitoring of children from the inappropriate places where they can be corrupted by a dangerous or bad company, is a modern practice. Space becomes important in limiting the children's actions, and safe places are at school, at home or in another space destined for children.

Spatiality is used as a means of controlling and restricting children in their experiences with the space. By placing children in classrooms in ordered rows, the teacher can exercise discipline and control using teaching facilities to organize the class into specific groups, doing certain activities in certain time periods. The child's playtime is limited spatially and temporally, with the child having to learn more about how and where to play, instead of playing freely interacting with other children without the supervision of an adult. By limiting himself at home, the child has no room to exercise autonomy, while at home he is under his parents' control. Childhood becomes a period of time that is spatially controlled both at home and at school.

The concept of "tabula rasa" (empty board) is the characterization of the human intellect at birth, according to the theory developed by the English philosopher John Locke (1632–1704). The philosopher describes the child's mind at birth as devoid of any knowledge, like a white sheet later supplemented through the senses, all we learn is the fruit of our experiences. The process of learning takes place during the development of the child, the skills and knowledge will be written on the tabula rasa, which will be filled with notions. "By following a child from his birth and observing the transformations that time is doing, you must see how through the senses, the mind becomes more and more filled with ideas, thus becoming more and more aware" (Locke, 1841). An important part of his theory was that education itself should not be unpleasant, educators should use methods adapted to the age of the child. The goal was to educate the child into a rational and responsible person with high morality. The concept of "tabula rasa" is an innovative concept in the field of philosophy, and is an attack on the doctrine of innate ideas. This theory that has a pedagogical and psychological foundation was one of the main sources of empiricism, and has greatly influenced the modern point of view on childhood.

Not by chance, Jean-Michel Vienne, in the new edition of the philosophical essay *Thoughts on Education* (1693) emphasizes that "Education, in Locke's eyes, is above all a moral one: it aims to train people who are aware of their dignity, with good habits, wise and more than educated. Locke belongs to this school of pedagogy, which places moral qualities above intellectual qualities. We see how important is the development of the will, the moral energy: *There is only one thing that can be kept well; without restriction, it is goodwill*" (Locke, 2007). Wisdom, which is the second essential quality of the child, consists in particular in theoretical knowledge, as well as in practice, and its source is experience. Therefore, raising and educating children is the responsibility of parents, and they should inspire their love for books and a desire to learn more and more. Locke is one of the first to attract educators' attention to the diversity of temperaments, both from a physical point of view, as well as morals. While maintaining the need for common rules for everyone, Locke wants the discipline or teaching methods to be adapted, in many cases, to suit the particular nature of the children.

This view of education is in contrast to the philosophical doctrine of experimentation, which does not admit that people have ideas with which they were born. He has always considered that the child brings with him personal interests and inclinations, and admits that nature is often stronger than education. "Nature has combined her works with such wisdom, she works in ways so far from our powers of discovery and our power of conception, that we will never be able to bring them back to scientific laws. Natural philosophy studies the principles, properties, operations of things, as they simply are" (Locke, 2007).

The romantic ideal of childhood, initiated by the great French philosopher Jean Jacques Rousseau, is based on the idea that children are naturally good, innocent and vulnerable and have the right to freedom and happiness. The postmodern interpretations in the educational space show the difficulty of the historical analysis of the concept. "In this situation, it must only be analysed the romantic movement that taking Rousseau's message, will end up by endorsing childhood as the happiest period of life, since it is the house of goodness," forgetting that the celebration of childhood as a symbol of innocence was not a new idea in the West. In fact, according to P. Riche's analysis, "there are more distant historical precedents that can be found in some of the pedagogical thoughts of monasteries at the beginning of the Middle Ages" (Giallongo, 1990).

According to Jean Jacques Rousseau, the inborn child's innocence must be preserved through careful education by applying child-friendly teaching methods. Childhood should be a time of play and pleasure, life should be enjoyed and play is the right and enjoyable activity for children. He equated childhood with nature, therefore with an innocent purity, and believed that the only way to get back to that kindness the child is born with is to be as close as possible to the nature. Nature was the natural teacher and the children are pure and innocent creatures close to God. "The man of the nature does not use reason; two fundamental feelings common to all animals direct his actions. The first commands him to pursue his own preservation: it is self-love; the second is the natural refusal to see another suffering sentient being: it is pity, that naturally moderates the actions that self-love will direct against others; it is the foundation of moral behavior, without being truly moral" (Guillaud & Lemoine, 2008).

The romantic vision of childhood attributed to the child a spirituality that brought him closer to God, nature and all good things. Rousseau equated childhood with nature and therefore innocent purity. He believed that the only way to get back to that kindness with which the child was born is to be as close to the natural environment as possible. The purity of the children should be respected and protected by the society that corrupts the child and separates it from nature (especially the separation between the nature of the child and its social environment). Rousseau uses a wall-like metaphor regarding the educational process and advises mothers to *build a fence* around the soul of the child, at an early age, to defend it from *the impact of human opinions*. To the extent that we have to correct these unacceptable inclinations, born of the impact with society, it is educational to say *no*:

"Your refusal to be irrevocable; don't let any enthusiasm move you; so that 'no' once pronounced, it will be a bronze wall against which the child can exhaust his power five or six times, but in the end he will not try to overthrow it. Therefore, you will make him patient, stable, calm and resigned even when he did not get what he wanted" (Rousseau, 1979).

Its purpose is to educate the child to become a natural man living in civil society, but never in the wild. The child cannot live in the forest with the bears to become a natural man. Rousseau described the corrupt social environment of his childhood in which the educational objective was only to satisfy the appetite for wealth and glory. Therefore the requirement is to conform to the goodness of human nature, while the child caught in his needs and desires is deviated from his good nature and is led on the path of vice. He prescribes a method favorable to the development of the child's natural dispositions. Since well-being is relative to the ability to satisfy our desires, true well-being can only be achieved through a balance between the child's desires and powers or faculties. Wanting less, rather than obtaining more, *without being tormented by unnecessary cravings* seems to be the key to contentment.

They should be protected by the society that corrupts the child and separates it from nature, and children should be allowed free development in friendly places according to their own needs and rhythms. Rousseau writes about childhood as a distinct period in the life of the child, as opposed to the spirit of the age when children were considered as miniature adults, who think and act as mature people. The way he builds the concept of education is quite revolutionary, and his theory of the nature of childhood being considered the foundation of modern education. There is a clear connection between the romantic view of childhood as a time of innocence and grace, and nature as the best place for children's lives and the educational model of outdoor kindergartens.

II.1 Educational theories about outdoor activities

The last years are marked by a change in certain aspects of educational content and the development of experiences toward a variety of new curricular concepts, even radical in content and organizational changes, such as creative education, ecological education and health education. What these concepts have in common is that they want to give children a new learning and living environment and adequate spaces for the needs of the contemporary child. Children need areas of experience that are stimulating, inspiring their curiosity and creative imagination. The natural living conditions have a special role in this context, we should be aware that education does not take place exclusively through direct contact between the child and the adult, because the physical environment has a considerable influence. Finally, it is often more effective to change the child's environment rather than trying to change the child.

There are a variety of teaching methods in preschool education. In this chapter, alternative pedagogical concepts of traditional preschool education are presented and analyzed. Pedagogy thus becomes an open-air pedagogy, using the natural space. Froebel pedagogy is the basis for today's education in kindergartens in Scandinavian and Western countries, the Montessori pedagogy is the most common in alternative educational approaches and the Nature pedagogy (Forest Pedagogy) originates in ecological education and emphasizes the importance of playing in fresh air.

II.1.1 The Froebel pedagogy

The discovery of the educational significance of the game for the early development of the child is the contribution of German pedagogue Friedrich Froebel (1782–1852). "Play is the highest level of child development, of human development at the moment; is a free representation of the interior, a representation of the necessity and the desire to perfect the Ego itself, regardless of the play of words, it expresses itself" (Fröbel, 1826). He founded the first kindergarten in 1840, and at the same time created a new profession for women – the kindergarten teacher. Even the name of kindergarten says everything; the early education of the child should be like a garden, a small paradise. Thus the children's kindergarten is a return of the children to Paradise, as in a garden under the protection of God and the care of experienced, understanding gardeners who keep plants in full harmony with the nature. From a historical point of view, the principles of the Freibellian pedagogy emerged in the middle of the eighteenth century – the Age of Lights (also known as the Age of Reason or simply the Enlightenment). Froebel's basic philosophical principles "absolute spontaneity and freedom, creativity, social participation and educational value of the game" started with a small idea, to become something important, a sustainable value. "Central to Froebel's thinking is the idea that education is about the relationship between self, others and the universe. These elements make up a whole and lead to an understanding and respect for the unity that is in all things. Nowadays we no longer describe this as 'unity.' Instead, we usually talk about the whole child" (Bruce, 2012).

According to Froebel, holistic education means the development of the whole personality of the child, emphasizing intellectual, emotional, social, physical, artistic, creative and spiritual development. Multilateral development varies for each child and is influenced by internal predispositions (biological abilities within the child) and external influences (physical and social). Froebel believed that education is a development from within, in which the life of man is enlarged, until it correlates with nature. Education has the role of revealing the child's innate powers and awakening its spiritual nature so that it can have spiritual union with God. It implies a deep respect for the integrity of the biosphere, if not a sense of reverence for nature.

Also, with regard to preschool education, he was the first to present a specific educational plan for early childhood (theoretical play) and put it into practice. He was the first to discover the meaning of a conscious (intentional) education and the opportunities that a large number of children provide for the common education. This connection to the concept of childcare and age-appropriate education makes the kindergarten concept brilliant. The Froebelian Kindergarten was inspired by the idea that through the collective play of parents and children, it will improve family behavior in the parent-child relationship. Froebel saw the family as the first stage of the parent-child relationship, and the second stage was the development of the children's kindergarten education. He admitted that in the process of parental love education, the maternal instinct is not enough. From his point of view, child development is divided into three areas:

– firstly, the play and play games (toys) and the game materials that are elements for self-expression. Conventional toys should complement and promote the child in its development,
– secondly, interactive games,
– thirdly, the gardening, which is a place of responsible practice.

At the kindergarten, each child is offered a small space where useful flowers and plants can grow. This gives the child an experience of growing and maturing plants, and the garden is the mirror of its development. The common goal of these activities is to illustrate the harmony between God, man and nature and constitutes a parable of human coexistence. The garden is a place to look, respect and recognize, a place for physical activity and to create its own ideas. His ideas were revolutionary through their pedagogical influence, being an exemplary model of international education alongside other theories, such as J. J. Rousseau's theory of child education, especially his point of view that man is good through nature and education.

II.1.2 The Montessori pedagogy

Maria Montessori (1870–1952) is seen as the most representative figure of Italian pedagogy in the last century. Her pedagogy is based on the principle of freedom as a daily practice, a pedagogy that made freedom its life vital. She has taken into account the idea of education by freedom, but a freedom to develop independence and autonomy using didactic strategies that do not ignore the free choice of children. "The fundamental principle of scientific pedagogy must undoubtedly be the freedom of the child; must allow individual development, the spontaneous manifestation of the child's nature. In case a new and scientific pedagogy arises from a person's study, such a study should deal with the observation of free children" (Montessori, 2002). She is focused on identifying new reference values to facilitate not only freedom of thought, but also creativity and beauty, for its symbolic value is the praise given to manual activities, "Praise to the Hand."

She believes that all education problems stem from the permanent conflict between the adult and the child, the obstacles to the child are numerous, serious and become more and more dangerous in the sense of leading them according to their own convictions. It highlights the "unconscious error and immense guilt" that resembles injustice at the roots of humanity, the adult being the one that causes the child's incapacity, confusion and rebellion, which vitiates the character of the child and represses its vital impulse. She emphasizes the concept of a child as a "living germ," an "active being," an "embryonic spirit."

The Montessori method is also called development education (help me to do it myself). The child works independently creates their own development following an internal plan. The educator knows the "plan" and only accompanies the child in the development stages, "sensitive periods" in which the child learns certain work determines its development. The Montessorian professor must especially know how to observe, not intervene at random or pushed by prejudices. The pedagogical method of observation is based on the freedom of the child and freedom is the activity that allows individual spontaneous manifestations. "Interesting encouragements are found at Maria Montessori, who saw the freedom of the child as the only condition to express their creativity, and who strongly supported the educational importance of the child's relationship with the nature" (Sofo & Calabrese, 2015).

In the Montessorian green schools, the outdoor classroom in the garden of the school is an important aspect of the educational model. The relationship with nature offers a variety of activities that aim at children's welfare, additionally know how to dig and seed, do gardening and raise animals. Child development and self-development can be encouraged by designing the educational environment, providing the means that lead to this development of freedom. Thus, natural stimuli, gracefulness and latent creativity in the child can be added to its individuality and initiative. It supports the necessity and opportunity for the educator to leave the child free and spontaneously express any potential that must be supported by an appropriate environment, where the new generations can "grow and sprung." The educational environment is particularly important to be stimulating, friendly and aesthetic, where toys, windows and shelves should be simple, accessible and adapted to children's size, room, furniture and building, influencing the personality of the child. Only in this context can the child freely express their own inclinations and interests with the aid of specially structured materials. Essentially, all children have an "absorbing mind" (the so-called cognitive function), which, if appropriately stimulated, facilitates an unconscious connection of data from the environment in which they grow. The pedagogy of the first female doctor in Italy is one of the major concepts of the European educational reform that emerged at the beginning of the last century.

II.1.3 Nature (forest) pedagogy

Nature (forest) education is part of the environmental education and is therefore related to education for sustainable development. Environmental education is primarily concerned with environmental issues, and so far has rarely been fully integrated into a general concept of education. Nature (forest) education allows for a practical learning experience and wants to create an understanding of ecological and social contexts, to demonstrate the biodiversity of nature by bringing the learning environment into the nature. "Education in nature or nature education is therefore the study of ecological methods and practices of working with nature and which are part of a set of values" (Warden, 2015). It aims to allow children to live actively and responsibly, Pestolazzi's holistic learning concept with the "head (mind), heart (emotion) and hand (action)" being the main pillar. It is important not to lose or prevent children from experiencing the nature, to awaken their love for nature. Learning and understanding through direct encounters with nature can be achieved through play, and free play offers optimal opportunities for sensory-motor development.

In the Western culture, nature is understood as what has emerged from itself, something that is not created directly by humans. Nature is always in relation to living organisms and is part of the environment. The concept of nature has been defined as the opposite of culture and the universal source of all phenomena. By nature, we understand a space with a particularly harmonious relief, mountains, valleys, meadows, forests and lakes, where we can find wildlife, gather mushrooms, forest fruits, environments that give us a good state and where we can pause the time in our lives.

The point of view of this educational approach is based on the belief that the environment experienced by the child places its mark on its knowledge and attitude, shapes its personality, values and basic identity. The natural environment is considered the third teacher and is structured autonomously. This autonomous structure corresponds to the philosophy of outdoor kindergartens, namely, free-to-imply learning. "The forest is not a space that is structured pedagogically and complemented with ready-made interpretations. However, for this very reason, it is an extremely interesting space from a pedagogical point of view. In the vicinity of wild places, the air has something provocative, sometimes scary, but also something that is comforting and protective, where one can hide and rest. This dual character very well meets the child's fundamental needs for something new on the one hand, and something familiar and comforting on the other" (Clipa & Boghian, 2015; Knight, 2013). In nature, there are different objects, phenomena, slow and rapid changes that can be perceived by the child in varying degrees of complexity.

Discontinuity and differentiation of natural places is a challenge for the child. Flexibility, adaptability, empathy and creativity are necessary if the natural differentiated space is discovered by the child day by day. Identity formation begins at birth and develops throughout life, being based on day-to-day actions and communication, which is also called the life story or experience. Walking in a certain part of the forest, keeping your balance on tree trunks and climbing in smaller trees promote creativity and communication. Children want to play together and communicate the meaning of adventures in nature. There is a very intimate relationship of children with nature, and that is why the existing childhood contacts are indispensable for a healthy emotional development. An emotional approach to environmental issues such as animal love, compassion and worry or fascination will develop the child's sensitivity to all forms of life. For preschool children are such places, including outdoor kindergarten, a place where children can identify themselves and where they spend years of living with a beneficial effect on physical, mental and spiritual development.

II. 2 Outdoor activities

II.2.1 Outdoor kindergarten – concept and context

"The Children's Kindergarten in the Forest is a creative process that provides for all those who regularly learn opportunities to achieve, develop self-confidence and self-esteem through practical learning experiences in a local forest or natural tree environment" (Knight, 2013). The outdoor (forest) kindergarten offers an alternative to preschool pedagogy using the natural environment for learning. It is an innovative form of education, where children always practice in the open air, there is no proper edifice of the kindergarten, and the children play in any kind of time, and only in particularly unfavorable conditions they go inside a shelter. The basic principle of this type of kindergarten compared to the traditional kind is the daily report of children with the nature, seen as a learning and living environment, entrusting to the cyclical rhythm of the seasons, as well as the absence of a building as their own residence.

It is well known that nature has a beneficial influence on the physical, mental and spiritual development of children. For this, the outdoor kindergarten is based on an educational concept that considers nature as an essential element for the healthy and multilateral development of children, and the forest is considered the best environment to meet these requirements. "A particularly interesting innovation is the rapid spread of the Wald-kindergarten phenomenon in the German-speaking countries of Europe: Germany, Austria and northeastern Switzerland. Wald-kindergarten literally means 'kindergarten in the woods.' These are kindergartens that have no building, no walls. Children meet the teacher in a local park or wooded area, every day, throughout the year. They can spend one or more days studying a dozen trees: examining every tree, playing in the leaves if it is autumn, learning about seasonal cycles and life cycles of these trees, building a swing from the branches on a secular shaft" (Sax, 2007). Decisive for its emergence was that the social and ecological environment has changed dramatically in recent years. Children have less space available for movement and play; green areas, "true islands of nature" have faded and the result is that more and more children have retreated to play in the apartments.

Outdoor kindergartens are becoming more popular in Western countries. Named Forest schools, nature schools and Naturbarnehage programs of this kind are generally aimed at urban children who have less contact with nature. In our country, there are currently kindergartens in the private sector that have such experiments in nature or even promote this concept. The term kindergarten in the forest and kindergarten in nature is often understood the same. However, there are significant differences between them. The kindergarten in the forest is about bringing the children in the nature, while the kindergarten in the nature pursues the idea of bringing nature to the kindergarten. This can be characterized by natural playgrounds, maintained or exploited: pastures, meadows, ponds, vegetable gardens and farm with its main attractions (hens, rabbits, sheep and ponies). These natural habitats, constructions and equipment are mainly developed from an ecological point of view.

Forests are a prerequisite for any kindergarten in nature, and where there is no forest, education takes place in other forms of environment. It is important to know that the forest is the most important natural habitat for humans and the children want to be close to the forest. However, a precise delimitation of these two types of kindergarten is not possible because many kindergartens in the forest call themselves kindergartens in nature, and the two pedagogical approaches resemble, constantly putting environmental issues into their work and having the same objectives.

II.2.2 The history of outdoor (forest) kindergarten

The idea of children playing in the open air in the Nordic countries has long been represented, early contact with nature being a prerequisite for the quality of life. Despite the unfavorable conditions due to the long and cold winter, education in nature has a long tradition. The history of pedagogy in nature dates back to the nineteenth century. Starting with 1892, the Swedish organization Friluftsfrämjandet launched educational activities for children throughout the year. In the neighboring country of Denmark, in 1954 Mrs. Ella Flatau designed and created the first kindergarten in the woods. In the day-to-day life, "she spent a lot of time with her own children and the neighbors," exploring the forest behind the house, thus awakening the interest and curiosity of other parents. "About 50 years ago, Ella Flatau founded Sollerod's first institution of this kind. She began by taking her own children, every day, in the forest so that they could play there and observe the nature. Some neighbors were interested and wanted Mrs. Flatau to take their children too, which she did. Interest has grown and so parents have jointly founded an initiative and eventually the first kindergarten in the forest. Today Denmark has over 60 outdoor kindergartens" (Rank, 2004). This first initiative proved to be the promoter of a new pedagogical trend that had a great popularity in several European countries. The main reason was that anyone can see the experience of joy shared when children play in nature and how they enthusiastically discover the world around them. Probably every child has a kind of "basic love" of nature. Love of nature is deeply rooted in the Norwegian culture. The Norwegian cultural practice is to spend a relatively large part of the day in nature and outdoors. Children in kindergarten "FriluftslivBarnehage, Naturbarnehage" take part in activities and games considered risky, which is considered to be amazing in countries outside Scandinavia. Friluftsliv literally means "outdoor life" but its real significance is much deeper; it is a state of mind and a way of life in these countries. "Friluftsliv expresses the idea that citizens in the Scandinavian countries will naturally want to connect with their environment in different ways and as often as possible" (Knight, 2013).

Ecological education programs allow children to have a practical learning experience that will create an understanding of nature's biodiversity, ecological and social contexts by bringing the learning environment into nature. "Outdoor education or education about nature is therefore the study of ecological methods and practices of working with nature and which are part of a set of values" (Warden, 2015).

It aims to offer children to live actively, responsibly, and Pestolazzi's concept of holistic learning, through all the senses "head (mind), heart (emotion) and hand (action)," is a main pillar. In order to understand the world both in its evolution and its ecological functioning, the great pedagogue argued for a holistic approach in the learning process. The concept of holism comes from the Greek concept of holon, which sees the universe as an indivisible structure, which cannot be reduced in parts. In Greek thought, above all, it was the unity of things (kosmos) and their mutual configuration. The ecological perspective is so important in today's holistic education that the term holistic is often used interchangeably with the ecological one. Holistic education tries to develop a pedagogy that is connected to the context and the environment and is in harmony with the cosmos. A main element of holistic education is to create a learning environment in which each child develops also from a spiritual point of view. Outdoor education supports the child's natural path of development and serves the purpose of connecting the child to something much bigger, beyond itself. It involves helping children to develop awareness that everything in nature forms a harmonious whole and that they themselves are part of and contribute to this whole.

"Nature designates, not a mechanism or a set of general laws, but a dynamic structure, an intelligible and immaterial principle of action, so a 'power' that should not be confused with the 'action' that derives from it, more than that, the invisible force must not be confused with the apparent movement" (Schulthess, 1996).

II.2.3 Forms of outdoor (forest) kindergartens

Almost all kindergartens in the forest (nature) are created by parents "initiative and depend on the state's recognition, the main objectives varying based of various initiatives of the parents' association. There are two different outdoor kindergarten types, the classic and the integrated model.

II.2.3.1 The classic kindergarten in the nature

"Constantly in all the institutions called 'authentic' or 'classical,' groups of children spend the whole morning in the nature, to a certain extent in a spatially limited area" (Kreher, 2008; Miklitz, 2000).

The particularities of these kindergartens are that they do not have their own building, the children being housed in a wagon on a wheel, designed as a living space located in the forest or at the edge of it. This shelter serves as a refuge for children and teachers when the weather is unfavorable (frost, storm and hail) and is also useful for sheltering various objects, tools, exchange clothes and a place for children to have a snack in the winter. Daily activities take place exclusively in natural areas such as forests, meadows, plains and seashores. Children spend the whole morning in the woods or in the middle of nature, and in the afternoon they are at home. They generally participate five days a week, four hours in the summer and three hours in the winter. The size of the group of children is usually made up of about twenty children aged 3–6, and for their supervision there are two or three teachers. In winter, when there are low temperatures, there is an alternative program such as reading shelters, handicraft, painting and museum visits.

II.2.3.2 The integrated kindergarten in the nature

"The integrated outdoor kindergarten has, in contrast, its own headquarters where the children go after a morning in the forest, more precisely in the afternoon are cared for as in a traditional kindergarten. The integrated outdoor kindergarten satisfies the needs of the working parents, their children being cared for throughout the day" (Lorber,

2012). This is a full-time kindergarten with a building and own rooms where the groups of children carry out their activities in the forest (nature). It was desired to create a care system that promotes the interest of the child and at the same time support parents working and wanting to bring their children to an outdoor kindergarten. Thus the widening of the educational concept has been achieved by combining the classical kindergarten model with the traditional kindergarten. The children spend the morning in the woods, and they go for lunch or rest in the classrooms in the afternoon, just like in a traditional kindergarten. This pattern is widespread in Denmark, Sweden and Norway, while in Germany the classic model prevails. There are different kinds of integrated outdoor kindergartens:

1. Outdoor kindergartens with a fixed group. In this model, a fixed group of children spend each morning in the forest for one month, then change with another group of children for the successive month. In the afternoon, they are cared for indoors as a traditional kindergarten.
2. Outdoor kindergartens with a flexible group. Here every child can decide on a daily basis if they participate in forest activities. In some institutions, there is a fixed schedule when children go to the forest or stay inside the kindergarten.

II.2.3.3 Other versions

There are various models to integrate the forest (nature) into the traditional children's kindergarten. For example, "weeks with activities in the forest" or "days when children are going into the forest." Weeks with activities in the forest take place over a period of one to three weeks, and the projects concern all topics related to nature and forest. Kindergartens that decide to spend specific days in the forest choose one day a week where children, in any kind of time, go to the forest.

II.2.4 Differences between traditional and outdoor kindergartens

The outdoor kindergarten in its classical form is fundamentally different from the traditional kindergarten. A home-like building does not exist; children play with the "wind and seasons" outdoors. Life in nature is linked to a cyclical time, rhythm of the four seasons, which allows children a close participation in the rhythm of nature. In nature, the possibility of movement and the space of action is significantly higher than in enclosed spaces in the classrooms. The possibility of having a direct relationship with a large natural space at this age urges children to live freely. The forest offers unlimited conditions for movement: children can climb trees, run and jump and "keep their balance on tree trunks." While kindergartens in the forest usually develop a full range of these experiences throughout the "outdoor all-time" educational approach, countless kindergartens in nature use two complementary strategies to achieve the same goal. One of these is "walking" with the whole class, exploring every day in wild places. [...] "The second strategy is to daily create a limited natural playground where every child is free to choose who he/she wants to play with, what activities he/she wants to do and how long he/she wants to spend with each game or responsibility" (Sobel, 2016). The values of independence, physical strength and resilience, perseverance, calmness, kindness, tolerance and mastery of difficult situations (the development of a robust and vigorous child in nature) are closely related to the values of nature and outdoor play. Children going to kindergarten in the nature are healthier, and they are skipping less because of illnesses than the children in less challenging environments.

Generally, nature is considered as a healing environment and spending time outdoors strengthens the body, the mind and thus the immune system. In nature, children get in contact with mud and dirt, the highly ozonated air, sometimes they get wet, and this strengthens the immune system and prevents allergies and contagious diseases that are so common in childhood. "Young children are genetically obliged to do this because it serves in the immunization process against local fauna and flora bacteria" (Sobel, 2016). Neglecting sensory and motor skills can have a negative impact on health. But health is more than physical exercise, and well-being and joy are just as necessary. Nature increases positive emotions, reduces stress, anger and frustration, and it does well not just to hyperactive children. The vastness of the space contributes to reducing the risk factors that sometimes may promote mental disorders manifested by behavioral disorders, such as learning or concentration deficit, aggressive and emotional disorders. Nature is a sensory stimulating environment, which leads to curiosity and could provide a living sense to children who want to improve their skills. "Natural areas are the perfect expression of this cognitive wealth – far beyond what even the best, more elaborate classroom indoors, can offer" (Sobel, 2016).

With regard to the use of toys, a particular feature is that toys are built with materials discovered in nature, such as stone, clay and wood. Apart from some equipment, pre-manufactured or purchased toys are not used here. Natural, ecological materials must give the child the opportunity to independently experience and develop their creativity. A creative mindset of learning needs new and varied stimuli, and the children using toys or the conventional games have little freedom to perform creative practical actions. It must be said that the conditions for the creative success consist of a relationship of self-confidence. The possibility of self-efficacy and self-confidence are some of the main goals in the educational work in outdoor kindergartens. They focus on enhancing the knowledge of professional life but also on preserving the traditional way of life. In outdoor (forest) kindergartens, children learn the respect for dangerous instruments by using them. The beauty is that everything happens through game and the game is fun. "The educational approach of the kindergartens in the forest considers the risk of being beneficial for the development of children, because it gives them a chance to experience their own limits, to work to expand the boundaries where possible, and to accept the limits that can not be extended" (Sobel, 2016). Kindergartens in nature must be recognized as a living space, all the requirements of everyday life are as much as possible made by children. Daily activities provide social resonance, children want to participate in the social life – cleanliness, cooking, gardening and trades where they have as much imagination and enthusiasm as playing. Here, the real work is the reward of the children; they can show that they do not need help, and adults do not undertake any activity that can be done by the children. The appreciation of children's activity is significant. They learn by mastering frustrated situations, through their own initiative or with the help of others, to develop self-confidence. In kindergarten, the class of children is significantly smaller than in the traditional kindergarten, at most 15–20 children who are cared for by 2 or 3 persons. Childcare is usually limited to a maximum of 6 hours, mainly in the morning. Most kindergartens have a wagon on the wheels as a shelter, in which the group can stay in case of unexpected weather conditions. This happens very rarely; usually the children are in the woods even in the rain, snow or cold. A kindergarten in the nature can offer this in very few places, being reserved for parents and very selective children. With the spread of this educational concept, the organizational structure changes and there are also integrated forestry gardens.

In the kindergarten in the nature, the natural development of the child, the play and social interaction are essential. Kindergartens in the nature put different accents and have different priorities, since there is not yet a common and binding concept. In the kindergarten in the nature, the development of social, sensory, motoring and environmental education skills is more prominent than the development of school-related skills.

II.3 Education through the outdoor activities and the impact for development of preschool's personality

II.3.1 Social education

The outdoor kindergarten in the nature (forest) is the basis for the development of social behavior, the skills acquired here influencing a child's whole life. "The responsibility of social skills is undoubtedly a primary objective in all kindergartens. As in traditional kindergartens, the kindergartens in the nature also have opportunities for movement – the possibility of free play, joint activities – in small groups as well as the alternative of individual play. Here they should learn, socialize, perceive their emotions and others', and help them properly, negotiate a fair compromise and conflict, take responsibility" (Dell Rosso, 2010). In nature, it is easier to work in relation to the needs of learning social skills. There is more space here that allows children free play, and therefore better communication between children, they learn to take care of each other and it is easier to bind a friendship here. In nature, dangers are overcome and experienced together. A strong sense of belonging develops within the group, children being often dependent on each other. Hiking is often used to give them the opportunity to cooperate.

There is nothing more special for children than walking in the woods. The youngest child goes to the front and determines the rhythm, while the older ones ensure that no one is lost, so they have to cooperate. If a stream of water is passed, a heavy log, a stone is overturned, or a slope is often reached, children need mutual help. This not only promotes social behavior, but also their communication with each other. Teachers usually talk with the children when they are in the woods, and have some rules. Children have to take care of each other and be sure everyone has someone to play with.

At the same time, there are children who are happier alone, or together with adults. In such a situation, the teacher helps children interact with each other and include them in the group of children. Social skills can be strengthened by enhancing children's well-being. The staff makes sure that they have a place to warm up, have their clothes dry and some food in their backpack for snacking. Because of the small group of children, the time spent paying attention to each child is higher, and misunderstandings can be resolved as quickly and constructively as possible. "Interaction among children is a fundamental experience in the early years of life. Interaction is a requirement, a desire, a vital necessity that every child secretly has" (Clipa, 2014a; Dahlberg et al., 1999). Children best interact if there is something they care about. Through play and outdoor activities, children are surprisingly cooperative, affectionate and independent. They learn the standards of positive interaction: to have patience, to be tolerant, to help and to assume responsibility for others, to know what is allowed and what is not allowed and to peacefully resolve non-violent conflicts. In this way, they are taken into account, which emotionally contributes to the quality of their lives, their colleagues and adults, and thus become responsible. The great need for children to move at this age unloads the aggressiveness, compared to the traditional kindergarten where restrictions and lack of space are factors in favor. In an age where aggression is a growing phenomenon, social education must be a major objective of childcare in kindergarten.

II.3.2 Sensory development

Children perceive the environment through the senses. During childhood, the development of perceptual experiences is the basis of all learning processes. Forest with its greatness, vastness and silence, the harmonious diversity of its habitat, provides optimal conditions for the sensory development of the child and stimulation of the learning process. The senses are the interface between the child and the world, and with their help they come in contact with the environment. "For children, sensory perception is the access to the world. It is the root of every experience, through which they will be able to rebuild and understand the world" (Rath, 2001).

There are several forms of perception: when the stimuli come from the outside, they are included in the remote senses, auditory (hearing), visual (sight) and olfactory (odor) or from the inside and outside of the body, gustatory (taste), tactile (touch), kinesthetic (sense of movement) and vestibular (sense of balance). There is also the emotional perception of relationships between people, or between people and the environment. Sensory development in the first years of life has a decisive role; children need a variety of sensory stimuli to develop positively. Children enjoy exciting sensory experiences such as speed, rhythm, sliding, rocking, climbing, rolling and rotation. This means taking risks, and they are constantly looking for stimuli, especially in terms of balance. "Nature in the forest does not only serve as a background for play and experiences, but its specific features and themes are also analyzed, for example the sensory qualities with its shapes and colors (light and shadow, trees or leaf shapes) or natural science topics (plants, roots, growth, gravity)" (Knight, 2013).

The physical challenge such as climbing trees includes an essential element – the sensory experience, both the tree in its environment is felt, and so does its own body, with its capabilities and limits (Dumbrava, 2016). Branches and leaves offer ideal conditions for balance, children learn about balance with their whole body, for example, by stretching their arms. Once children are safer on the ground, they are looking for new challenges that promote coordination and concentration: higher slopes, tree trunks and higher roots for climbing. Their imagination has no limits, in their free play they can discover different ways of balancing and jumping over rocks. Appealing to the child is especially the overcoming of all types of altitude. The challenging physical exercise has a decisive contribution to their physical and mental well-being. "This knowledge is used in a sensorial way to develop children's learning independently, through their own discoveries" (Knight, 2013). A child is exploring his environment "step by step," and his movement should be as varied and stimulating, and his long-lasting outdoors is preferable to enclosed spaces. The outdoor kindergarten provides an excellent environment for all sorts of such innovative moves, especially in the forest with the vastness of its space. The forest is a living space and the children live in it. Here, no day is the same because the weather and the seasons always change the environmental conditions. Diversity is something to be perceived; there is always an abundance of landscapes, sounds, smells, touches and sensational real movement through a direct encounter that awakens emotions in every child. Insect bruising, bird twittering, leaf rustling, a squirrel squirming in the branch, the stars in the sky, and the sounds of the forest are enthusiastic, yet children's senses are not overstimulated. Nature with its vivid experiences offers a variety of opportunities and is an excellent environment in which children can develop holistically.

II.3.3 Motor development

Nowadays, there is a lack of management of children's contact with nature or the animals, of free play without the adults' supervision and control. Many children have not learned how to walk long distances, they consume much but do not move. The consequences of the lack of movement are the spread of abnormal, pathological hyperactivity or depression contrast, along with sedentary diseases. To these phenomena do the outdoor kindergartens try to give an adequate answer? "Twenty-one-year-old children spend an average of eight hours a day interacting with digital media and thirty minutes a day outdoors. The outdoor kindergartens and the kindergartens in the forest are an attempt to restore a healthy balance between indoors and outdoors in children's lives" (Sobel, 2016).

The relationship a child has with the nature should not only be virtual, but must also involve physical activity and senses, so that it is a real experience. In an outdoor nursery, movement is a necessity and every child can live up to his inborn urge to move, to seek the challenges of his age. The basic concept of kindergarten in the nature is that outdoor living is the ideal place for children to develop, which fulfills their biological need to move. Many developmental factors of the child are genetic, and in his development, the child requires perception and movement.

In traditional kindergartens, children spend most of their time seated in desks in the classroom, under the guidance of the teacher. Lack of space and movement are reflected in the children's behavior. Having less space available, misunderstandings and confrontations in the group of children are more common. The teaching is done in the classroom without giving space to creative experiences, to allow children to express their joy and be physically active. Teachers have vague notions about outdoor learning, they are not aware of the educational role of these situations. The forest on the other hand offers plenty of space, but children can run faster and more, they can climb into shrubs, bounce and use the body freer. A quiet place can be found when it is necessary to avoid the occurrence and escalation of conflicts. Ideal for motor activity are higher slopes, trenches, valleys, trunks of trees, roots, climbing on cliffs or among the tree branches and leaves. "The freedom to move unattended in the environment around gives the child the opportunity to connect with the nature (such as catching tadpoles in a watercourse) to have adventures and learn from their experiences and mistakes (for example, trees that are safe or unsafe for climbing), play imagination games with friends and enjoy being active and inexperienced" (Beaulieu, 2008).

Physical activity develops the entire personality of the child, including linguistic and cognitive abilities. While children use their body and experience a variety of motor skills, they learn the meaning of terms. Thus, they lay the foundations for mathematical understanding, can compare the size of stones, leaves, different shapes, a crooked stick, an oval stone, and get a concrete understanding of the terms. By talking about what they discover, they develop their language, children have to explain, listen and be patient, and they explore and acquire certain knowledge of nature and its conceptual understanding. The motor skills of children playing in natural environments such as the forest are greatly improved. These children perform tests of concentration or physical training. Children have a natural need for the world around them, which they want to understand, research, and experience. They need an environment that they can touch, feel, hear, smell, and where they can move and gain experience. Without this development of the movement, an independent, self-confident and healthy adult personality is almost impossible to achieve. The experience of movement can be regarded as a basic principle of an evolutionary, physical, mental and spiritual life.

II.3.4 Education for the environment

Today's children are becoming more and more stressed and demoralized, and the causes of this phenomenon must be searched in the way they spend their time between the four walls of the house, in cities affected by urban traffic, where both green spaces and their parents' free time are insufficient. There are children who do not know the trees, the animals, but through media, lacking a fundamental part of knowledge, based on experience. "Human existence is conceived to take place simultaneously on two levels, the interpersonal social level, the relationship between people, and the natural ecological level of the organism's interaction with its environment, considering that the existence of the animals is entirely limited within the natural domain. A human being is at the same time both a person and an organism, all creatures are organisms" (Ingold, 2000).

In our technological world, the outdoor kindergarten, through its versatility, offers multiple opportunities and a lot of space for direct contact of children with the nature, and thus counteracts its estrangement or the degradation of the natural environment. The educational concept of the outdoor kindergarten (forest) is part of the education for the environment, and is therefore related to education for sustainable development. The field of environmental education is very broad, but children associate the term "environment" automatically with the "forest," that is of particular importance to them. Environmental education deals with specific environmental issues, such as waste prevention, waste separation, waste of energy, etc. It primarily concerns the ecological aspects and is value-oriented; it refers to life, and respect, moderation and humility are associated with it. Values are formed through experiences and the models in which we trust. Through a playful and cognitive approach, educators make nature accessible to children and they begin to be part of the relationship with them. It is usually assumed that direct experiences in the nature lead to an ecological behavior, but little attention is paid to the inner experiences.

An emotional approach to environmental issues such as animal love, mercy, worry and fascination will develop the child's sensitivity to all forms of life, to himself and to others. "Empathy between the child and the natural world should be a primary objective for children aged between four and nearly seven years old. As children begin their incursions into the natural world, we can encourage feelings for the creatures that live there" (Sobel, 2016). Understanding nature as something that has to be specifically protected, must lay the foundations for a responsible attitude to the age of maturity. Sustainable education can take place if children's sensitivity and sensory understanding of nature develops. In the outdoor kindergarten, the awareness and education refers to plants, animals, seasons, nature and natural materials, social behavior of waste prevention, fantasy and story characters.

Knowing the nature and the awareness of children's responsibility for the environment and becoming familiar and acquiring an understanding of plants and animals, seasons and climate are issues in the learning process. This involves the love of nature and the understanding of the interaction between man and nature. Being responsible for the natural environment is to help preserve nature. The interest in everything that fascinates us cannot save the natural environment alone, but it is a necessary element for protecting and preserving only what we love. For this reason, environmental education must be carried out in places characterized by the richness of natural resources, such as natural parks, the forest, thus developing an emotional attachment to the place.

II.3.5 Organization and daily activities

Kindergarten activities in the forest (nature) take place in the morning, for about four hours, five days a week in both summer and winter. Children perform all outdoor activities even when it is raining or snowing, according to the dictum "there is no bad weather, only inappropriate clothes." Everyday life in the kindergarten is special, and opening hours are usually between the hours eight and nine. Children are brought by their parents to the meeting place agreed, with cross-compatible means of transport because, given the proximity of nature, this educational concept excludes other means.

The appropriate clothing during summer is long trousers, long-sleeved shirts and sun hats as standard, and a multi-layered chemise is required in the winter. Each child has comfortable shoes, waterproof pants and a raincoat at hand. The daily companion of the children is a backpack containing a snack, a water thermos and a cup and a rug for thermal insulation. Children bring the morning snack from home, in a backpack, which is mainly made of fruits, vegetables, bread and cereals, while sweets are not recommended. "It is an opportunity for parents to inform teachers about the events that took place in the lives of children outside school" (Sobel, 2016). After the children say goodbye to their parents, they form the morning circle which is a welcoming symbol of the beginning of the day. The activities within the circle are greeting between children and teachers, determining who is missing, welcome songs and poems, different motion games, discussions about the experiences of the previous day. "Teachers form a circle. Holding our hands, we say a blessing, we sing a song or share what happened during the day. We light a candle and honor the time whenever possible, especially if we have a busy week, keep the school family in our hearts, or we have difficult events on the horizon" (Sobel, 2016). After a short break, children and teachers go out into the woods. In the protected areas, a permanent consultation and cooperation with the forester is required. Teachers are equipped with a backpack and a hand-held stroller for emergency situations, containing: a cellphone, a first aid kit, a rain tent, a drinking water or warm tea container, exchange clothes, utensils for DIY, towels, soap and other materials such as books to identify all plants and animal species. There is no rush here, children have their own walking pace and they can make between one and three kilometers a day.

While on the move, children are free to run, but those who are in the avant-garde are waiting for the rest of the group at the crossroads, and only when the last child is there, the movement continues. They are stimulated to explore the forest, collect leaves, sticks, stones and other "treasures," to observe the animals they meet. "Small children spontaneously encounter animals and animal families and then associate their own life with the animals" (Sobel, 2016). On the way, breakfast is allowed to children, allowing them time according to the dictum. "The trip is the destination." For breakfast, a suitable location is found and the mattresses (carpet) are very good in the winter. Reaching the pre-set place, the free game takes place under the supervision of the teacher who intervenes only if strictly necessary. Every child plays freely, some play in pairs, others in a group, and others play alone in the natural environment. "Teachers notice, but only intervene if there are dangers that children do not see – thus increasing the probability of risk benefits.

Group communication, personal adaptability and a growing understanding of nature are some of the positive benefits of risk that are worth mentioning" (Sobel, 2016). At mid-morning, after the bell signal, they call the children for the second snack. Children wash their hands in the pool of water that is brought every day, and then they sit in a circle and can quietly begin to eat together. After the snack, there is a free game play and activities conducted by teachers where each child can choose whether to participate or not. These can take the form of fantasy games, stories, songs, handicrafts, carving and cutting wood, working with clay, creating a herbarium and exploring the nature. Eventually, the group goes back to the meeting place and end with the farewell circle. The way back seems longer and the faces of the children can sometimes look fatigue. Generally, children are back in kindergarten from 12 to 13 o'clock, where parents take them back home. In addition to the usual hiking, children also visit the forester, the fire department, museums.

Children's clothing is one of the many aspects of childcare where staff and families share responsibility because clothes can affect their health, safety and comfort. Clothing can provide protection against dangers and inclement weather, support or prevent participation in certain activities and can be a key issue in individual expression. Since no season is without rainfall, clothing for outdoor living depends on the weather conditions.

Participation in outdoor activities requires knowledge of codes of conduct regarding the use of exclusive clothing and equipment. Clothing is an important investment for the benefit of our children. Instead of many cheap clothes, it is better to buy quality clothing that is environmentally labeled. Clothes often have different coating layers with different chemical compounds that are not disclosed and that can be absorbed into the body. Children may be very sensitive to skin irritant tissues, and some may have an allergic reaction to some prophylactic clothing treatments. To keep the baby warm and comfortable there should be additional sets of clothes: wool sweater, wool socks, wool gloves and woollen underwear. The lack of changing clothes can cause limitations during the game regarding what children can do, for example, when they want to play in a puddle. The most popular clothing among children who play outdoors is woolen underwear. The clothes should fit properly, without being too loose or tight, be light and provide warmth, allowing children to move freely and comfortably.

"Although people need more utensils and clothing when going outdoors in winter than in other seasons, they do not have to buy a lot of fancy and expensive winter clothes to stay comfortable. The following basic layering principles can help anyone dress for the cold weather outdoors. When planning what to wear outdoors in cold weather, think in terms of the three Ws: moisture absorbent layer, warm layer and a weather layer (wind and water)" (Foran, Redmond & Loeffler, 2016).

In all four seasons of the year: in the cold of winter, in the power of wind and autumn mud, in the melting snow of spring and on sunny summer days, wearing more layers of clothing helps us keep our body temperature and reduce the risks associated with the weather. All it entails is the combination of a few clothing items for outdoor activities, so that they can be quickly and easily adapted to a variety of weather conditions.

When we go hiking, it is best to wear layers rather than wear a thick or bulky coat. It is important to have three layers of air between the outer garment and the body because only air can be thermally insulated. The inner layer that is directly on the skin should be thin, tight and made of wool, avoiding cotton underwear. The wool warms even if it is moist; the wool breathes so that the skin becomes airy and dries faster. Cotton is not suitable for heat because it stops the moisture in the clothes and the child's chance to freeze increases significantly. The children are very much on their backs, and together with their heads, the back is where they cool off most easily. Most children use a wool sweater as a middle layer because it provides enough heat when hiking in the woods. Finally, the outer layer is a windproof and waterproof material while breathing (by releasing water vapor).

For the environmental educator it is a simple matter to know if the child is cold – the hands and feet often provide a good indication of how the rest of the body is. We must not forget that the hands and feet are the most exposed body parts, and it is important to stay warm. In order to face the freezing weather with a minimum of equipment in winter, a multilayered windproof suit is mandatory. In spring and summer, it is important for all children to be protected from ticks, insect bites and sunlight. Suitable clothing in summer is long pants and long-sleeved shirt. A good sun hat on the head must also be windproof. Much of the heat loss of the body occurs through the head, so hats are important. Each child has comfortable shoes, waterproof trousers and a raincoat at hand. Regardless of the season, children need above all, sturdy footwear. Children use well-padded plastic boots with wool socks for spring/summer/autumn/winter that are waterproof and can be worn throughout the year. In addition, they can change two pairs of shoes, for example light hiking shoes that sit much better on the foot, breathe and give better foot hygiene than synthetic materials. In outdoor kindergartens, being responsible for a child is different from taking care of yourself, the requirements are higher when it comes to children's clothing.

There are numerous educational situations during a half day spent in nature. One of the most important activities is the time of breakfast, even snacks or lunch, related to the topic of food education. It is well known how much our health depends on a healthy diet, capable of bringing all the necessary nutritional components to the human body. Proper nutrition becomes essential for children, especially at preschool age. The supply of energy, in the form of calories derived from food, allows the development of the brain and the growth of organs, skeletons and muscles, strengthening the immune system. Eating not only satisfies the feeling of hunger, it is a complex cognitive act, it includes the pleasure of tasting and the joy of being together, or the nourishment for the soul, which has a beneficial effect on the state of mind. The tactile sensations, a handshake, the gaze, the words, nourish the soul and respond to the child's need for love and the desire to be "wanted" (recognized empathically and welcomed). The aspect of socialization and conviviality, the unifying character, is probably the central pillar that supports the moment of serving the snack and lunch in the kindergarten. This becomes an unusual and spectacular ritual, in which, often, the *social function* of serving snacks or lunch is stronger than its nutritional value.

In fact, before the meal, children sit in a circle, sing small songs and say poems that urge them to seek silence. Indeed, in silence they can learn to listen to the nature, voices and sounds they otherwise ignore, that silence that allows them to understand the flight of a bird or the birth of a flower. "For example, on the same day as referred to above, meal time and informal chatting are disrupted and a child learning subject is constructed when the following happens: Suddenly one of the staff members jumps up, bursting out: 'There's our squirrel!' He points toward a tall tree and several children jump up too, and the adult begins to ask questions: 'Does anyone know which color the squirrel has at present?' One of the children answers: 'Gray-brown?' 'Yes, that is correct,' the adult confirms, and asks more about which color the squirrel has during the summer" (Kjørholt & Qvortrup, 2012).

When it comes to food education, we need to create a calm and familiar environment, where children are more open to dialogue, gradually developing their perception of themselves and the feeling of being together with others. By having lunch together, the child comes into possession of knowledge that allows him to make the connection between the consumption of food and the person. It is obvious that they are told, how much of each food they should consume, that it is a healthy choice to eat fruits and vegetables rather than fried potatoes. It also happens that they try to make simple cakes, candies and biscuits. In this way, they learn to get their hands dirty, developing new simple recipes, even in complete autonomy. Selecting the ingredients, understanding the order and sequence of steps, manipulating the food and weighing it, helps to develop cognitive skills and fine motor skills. And this, of course, involves the availability of explaining good hygiene practices, the tools needed for the recipe being prepared, the ingredients needed to prepare healthy and nutritious food.

Since children will understand empirically by observing the coexistence of others, regarded as a model, it is essential that the teacher has an appropriate behavior in this regard. The teacher should eat in a visible position, suggesting to the children a positive behavior pattern. Each child begins to eat, and he spontaneously imitates the teacher, showing interest and curiosity about the grown-up food. We need to explain to them why we eat, and what is the importance of a varied diet, we do not have to be nutritionists to know these things. Therefore, children need to understand that the World of Food exists, learning about the World by recognizing the main foods. And to help them, we say that there is a pyramid that is not in Egypt, called the Food Pyramid. Our doctors have built it so that we become aware of all the foods that are the basis of a balanced and healthy diet. It reproduces in pictures the qualitative and quantitative needs of the body. From the point of view of their use, foods are grouped into five basic families: 1. Cereals and derivatives, 2. Legumes and vegetables, 3. Fruits, 4. Milk and derivatives, 5. Meat and other sources of protein, such as fish, eggs; the top of the pyramid is represented by fats and sugary products.

Given their young age, we cannot talk about the meaning and significance of feeding methods (the food chain), the story of the plant and animal kingdom from where the food comes. Therefore we will make a symbolic interpretation of the two "kingdoms" with the Fairy of Flowers and Fairy Fauna. Children in contact with nature will understand by direct observation what foods the Fairy of Flowers (flowers, fruits, cereals and vegetables) offers, and which the Fairy Fauna (milk, eggs, meat and fish), learning to introduce them into their diet. Some kindergartens provide a space where the child can grow in contact with the animals, the vegetable garden and everything that the farm environment can offer, in a context of productive activities. It is an education in direct contact with the rural world that teaches respect for nature and animals. Proposes a common activity in the kitchen, which starts from the care for the vegetable garden to the cooking product, ready to be eaten. Diet is closely related to the philosophy of agricultural farms, recovering the concept of seasonality, which means eating fresh produce according to the season. We could define the seasonality as the period of life of the fruits and vegetables when their nurseries are at their maximum and the taste is better. The food, much appreciated by children, is always based on organic products, purchased from the farm around the corner.

In conclusion, we can say that the preparation of simple foods, with what the children have harvested, eating cherries, taking a carrot, even eating fresh pork, is a philosophy of sustainable ecological consumption. In nature, there is not a single food, a universal food, that meets the complex nutritional needs of the human body. Therefore, it is important to take the widest possible variety of foods, to supplement the nutritional deficiencies of each food product. This organic, seasonal food is suitable to meet not only the needs of the body, but also the sense of taste, smell or sight through which happiness, joy and calm can be transmitted. Touching the freshest product in the garden, the child comes into contact with the unique aromas, smells and colors, plants sown and cared for even by the "small farmer," who, later, could cook them in salads or even desserts.

Choosing products of animal origin, such as eggs and milk, gives the child the opportunity to see how these animals live, becoming more aware and respectful of everything they eat. The growth rate of a child, the psychological and emotional development and the development of motor skills are influenced by how much and what they eat. Emotional stress can influence the intake of food and nutrients ingested. What is meant by nutrients? The popular answer: nutrients are the bricks that make up the food, present in different proportions, depending on the foods that the child consumes. The scientific answer is found in practically every biological discipline: "nutrient" means any substance essential for growth and the maintenance of life; these are proteins, lipids (fats), vitamins, mineral salts and water. By food, we mean a substance that contains nutrients released during the digestive process. "The most important of the current nutrients has been considered to be protein. This occurs most abundantly in animal foods – meat, fish, eggs and dairy products, and in the dried legumes, such as beans and peas. Butter and lard are exceptions to this statement, as they represent the fat of milk and meat. The proportion of protein present in meat and fish varies greatly with the kind and cut" (Atwater, 1910).

The energy requirement of the body is different from child to child, depending on age and level of physical activity. In order to manage physical activities optimally, it is absolutely necessary for all children to eat a consistent breakfast, such as milk with biscuits, cereal flakes, jam or honey bread, fresh fruit and yogurt. The snack should be varied from day to day, even to facilitate digestion, and may consist of fresh fruit, jam and honey, fruit juices, homemade cakes. Consumption of foods high in fiber, such as bread, rice and other whole grains, along with green vegetables, fruits and legumes, helps to increase the feeling of satiety. A preschooler should be guided in choosing foods that will satisfy his nutritional needs.

Childhood preferences, such as eating fruit and vegetables, can become good habits that last a lifetime. "Kids develop lots of eating habits, and they do it very early on. Some habits are obvious. If your child always drinks milk first thing in the morning or always insists on snacking from the same Backyardigans bowl, it is clearly a habit. Other habits are more subtle: When kids insist on eating a diet of peanut butter and jelly sandwiches, hot dogs, and chicken nuggets (but only one particular brand that they like), they have a habit. When they skimp on meals and then demand snacks, they have a habit. When kids say, 'I like it' before they even took a bite, a habit, too" (Rose, 2014).

Foods are not divided into "best" and "worst" but the concept of proportion (quantity of food consumed) is taken into account; another concept is to pay attention to those that need to be consumed in moderation (salt, sugar and fat), and finally there must be the concept of variation in nutrition. The person caring for a child should cook different dishes, by virtue of providing a diversified and nutritionally balanced diet. For the child who practices physical activity, through the sweat, the body releases large amounts of fluid, which leads to possible dehydration. To eliminate the danger of dehydration it is necessary to remember to drink an adequate amount of water. Water plays an essential role in the digestion, absorption, transport and use of nutrients and is the main means by which the toxic substances are eliminated. Among the various correct eating habits, the benefits of preparing food in a family context must be known. The food is tasty, authentic and healthy, ready to be brought to the table, only before being served. Lately, food models that are proposed by advertising messages, reflect commercial interests, rather than spreading a paradigm about healthy and fair eating. Eating is a daily activity that unites man with nature, with the real world. Packaged and canned foods, labelled and industrialized, raise questions, which can turn into sources of concern. If we return to being aware of the fact that *Food is an agricultural act*, we will inevitably be concerned about the well-being of current and future generations, and therefore of nature, of that place that hosts us and allows us to exist.

II.3.6 Education for dangers in the nature

Although the experience of nature involves certain hazards such as forest fruits and poisonous mushrooms, wasps and other insects, tinea from the foxes, flowing waters, children have a better protection against infectious diseases. Health risks are small due to the fact that through multiple possibilities of movement, hazards are better assessed. Here, from the first day of kindergarten, they learn that hygiene is an important thing and strictly follow the rules of injury prevention. "The risks of in-game play are minor compared to many other hazards that children usually experience, but what about benefits? The research has found a remarkable range of positive effects on the benefits of unstructured free play, the diversity of the natural framework – exactly the kind of experiences that the outdoor kindergartens and kindergartens in the forest provide. These benefits cover the whole area of the child's multilateral development" (Sobel, 2016). In a kindergarten in the forest, it is necessary to protect the children from different weather conditions, such as storms. In principle, the bad weather is not a problem because the children are dressed properly. When there are storms, there is the risk of being hit by a lightning. Although the storms in the early hours of the morning are rare, educators need to be trained. Since lightning is attracted to trees or high rocks, those must be avoided. A better protection if offered by the open areas, valleys or even in the middle of the fields. During a storm, in the woods there is a risk of overturning trees, or broken branches being taken by the wind, especially in winter when the frozen branches break easily. In large openings or in young forest areas, the danger of releasing branches is much smaller, and in winter, there can be no snowfall.

"The educational approach of the kindergartens in the forest considers the risk to be beneficial for the development of the children, because it gives them a chance to experience their own limits, to work on extending the limits where possible, and to accept the limits that cannot be extended" (Sobel, 2016).

Nature has a great influence on the lives of children and they feel grateful because they learn to love and understand nature from childhood. Playing in nature involves a lot of physical activities that are fun and inspire fear at the same time. An issue regarding the health of the children has to do with the incidents during playing in nature and outdoors. In kindergarten, children participate in several categories of games designed to assess their own abilities and avoid excessive risks, which have a real probability of causing bodily harm. These activities mimic the risks of real life through exciting forms of physical play that stimulate curiosity, discovery, deep focus, fear and joy. For this reason, minor bruises and scratches are considered as something that contributes to learning about the risk of injury (seen as a way of learning from their mistakes). The risky game is related to a vigorous physical activity, in particular:

1. Games at high altitude. It involves a real danger of personal injury falling from a high altitude: trees, rocks or other high places, such as slides, swings, sheds and the roof of playgrounds. Children love all forms of altitude and their desire to climb is found to be the main risky activity available. Playgrounds should provide any kind of activity for climbing, and the topography of many kindergartens has many natural features, such as a steep hill that is great for sledding, trees, tree trunks and rocks, providing opportunities for risky play.

2. Playing at high speed (uncontrolled speed and pace that could lead to collisions). Uncontrolled speed on bicycles or toys with wheels, slides or when children run, ski, sledge and skate (where they can learn how to walk in deep snow or ice) can give children the most risky activities, because of the high speeds.

3. Playing with dangerous instruments. Children learn to carve, chop and cut with scissors and saw or use a regular knife during meals or a knife to make a wooden toy.

4. Playing near a dangerous environment (such as water and fire). Fire is an endless source of fascination, but it is also useful for coping with the realities of life. When children are near a fire (cooking food out in the open flame, campfire and fireworks) they must understand that it is not a toy and is a dangerous element that must be used with great care. The water teaches children to understand, through their experiences, how precious it is for humans, plants and animals, when they see thirsty plants or when they leap for joy through the puddles of water. Water play is considered risky when children could fall into the water of a fast-flowing river or play in deep water (ponds and lakes) or near frozen water.

5. Rolling and falling games. Disordered games with physical activity such as drifting, fighting for fun where children can interact with each other usually take place between friends and is not seen as an aggressive form of play. It may involve the use of twigs or other objects with

which children are dueling one another, and the rule is that you should not strike. For example, the war with snowballs, or when a wooden stick can be a sword or a weapon, and a puddle can be a whole sea.

6. Games in places where children can get lost (playing in unknown, unrestricted areas). Children prefer places where they can hide (shrubs), trees and shrubs where they can live and do something attractive; an expression of this is that they build huts and shelters where they can be housed.

It's part of the nature of children to explore the world around them through play. Children will learn what is risky and what is safe and will improve their perception of risk, which will help them to master the risky situations. Taking risks during the game seems to be normal in the growing up of children. Even the little ones like to launch themselves into the sky in the banal wooden cradle, which gives them a sense of freedom difficult to understand when they are with their feet on the ground. They seek the joy of discovering and exploring their own limits, expressed as a combination of fun and courageous actions to dominate their own fear. It is essential to succeed in recognizing and accepting one's own competencies, if necessary beyond the limits of one's own capacity.

Risky play is an ambivalent activity because the emotions it provokes are joy and fear at the same time (*cheerful fear*). Children have their individual sense of risk and will seek challenges tailored to their own limits based on their own competencies and previous experiences. The personality and emotions of each child will influence the perception of the child, and the characteristics of the environment prove to be decisive in influencing the child's play. The educators stress the importance of the environment in the development of the child, which establishes a personal relationship with the playgrounds and hiking. "The characteristics of the playground (height, unstable surface and slope), that can produce a reasonable level of inconvenience and damage in the child's play, are crucial." It is important that you help the children in your care to develop their understanding of safety, which is a many-layered thing.

In part, it is about self- awareness. Where do I start and finish?, what can my body do? and how well can I control my actions? are questions that we see the tiniest babies wrestling with as they grasp at toys and develop their mobility'(Knight, 2011).When the child interacts with the world around him, the various systems of spatial, bodily and motor representation contribute to the awareness of his personal identity. Self-awareness, understood as the feeling of identifying one's own body and abilities, is stimulated in a natural environment. The child finds his own resources and abilities when he manages to put his strength to the test in a natural environment, such as a forest. Being confronted with the elements of the outer world helps him to understand what are the real physical limits of the body, risking without exaggerating, but without underestimating his own potential.

"... The teachers observe, but only intervene if there are dangers that children do not perceive – thus increasing the likelihood of the benefits of the risks. Group communication, the ability to adapt personally and an increasing understanding of nature are some of the positive benefits of the risk worth mentioning" (Sobel, 2016). As the teacher has an empathetic understanding of risk (listening to the voices of children), he is responsible for the needs and limitations of the child, in his need to face the risk. Involving the teacher in taking risks while the child is playing will act as a filter, not allowing the reckless actions that put the child in danger. The child needs guidance and the teacher can help him/her to recognize the serious risks and teach them about safety, such as when using dangerous objects for the first time. Through a trust-based interaction, the teacher helps him/her learn to face the dangers, sometimes more than the parents, in order to eventually be accepted as a member of the children's community. This is why he should feel like a bigger kid himself (Gilbertson et al., 2006).

II.3.7 Nature – a therapeutic factor

A famous message from the Hippocrates of Kos says that "A wise man should regard health as man's greatest joy and learn how, in his mind, to take advantage of his illnesses." Social-emotional health in modern society is considered a minor issue. A possible solution for behavioral disorders is to use nature's healing *power*, in order to improve the quality of life by reducing stress. Conducting therapeutic activities in nature stimulates memory skills, reduces aggression, including panic disorder, depression, some conditions as a result of childhood stress. The reason for this behavior must be sought in the loss of contact between the child and nature, that principle that we have always called *mother nature*. The answer may be paradoxical, but all children equally seek to reduce stress in places where there is contact with nature.

Our body is supported by three "large" systems – the nervous system (brain, spinal cord and senses), the endocrine system (hormones) and the immune system (spleen, spinal cord, lymph nodes and monocyte activity). No one tells us that these three complex "cognitive" systems, whose balance depends on our health, are influenced not only by natural phenomena, but also by plants, food, gestures, words, hugs, laughter or songs (laughter strengthens the immune system, the hug has a strong antidepressant effect). The achievements of molecular biology have shown, among other things, that even a single nerve cell responds to certain external stimuli (duration of illumination during the day, phases of the moon, temperature), which could bring benefits to health problems. On the other hand, neuroscience points out that nature offers emotional support, especially during the first three years of the child's development, and permanently throughout life.

Nature acts on the nervous system like a therapist, if, unfortunately, the discomfort manifests itself in our life. "Nature and outdoor life protect us as a shield against the negative effects of stressful situations. The vastness of the space contributes to the reduction of risk factors, which can sometimes promote the appearance of mental disorders manifested by behavioral disorders, such as: learning disorders, concentration, aggressive and emotional. Nature can be used as therapy for children with difficulty concentrating or hyperactive behavior. The physical exercise in the open air gives them a healthy fatigue, the manual activities also help them to get out of the hectic rhythm of daily life. Among the benefits of natural therapy we can mention the effects of volatile substances of the trees. Their leaves represent a true garden that is highly sought after, especially for the composition of volatile aromatic substances, which stimulate our senses so much" (Cîmpan, 2018).

Children with a strong naturalistic intelligence have the ability to recognize and classify natural materials of plant, animal or mineral origin. Such a predisposition – today defined today by the term *biophilia* – comes from the innate attraction that people feel towards other living beings.

This predisposition is clearly visible at preschool age; children are fascinated by the natural world, insects and animals.

Nature is capable of stimulating the child's learning at the sensory, cognitive and linguistic levels, and is also capable of stimulating creativity. Learning comes from a direct contact of the child with nature, which uses the external environment as a real classroom. The nature in which it has *dipped* allows it to understand mainly, the phenomena in which animals, plants, microorganisms and non-living substances are linked in a complex fabric, on which our lives depend. All medical research shows that children's health (physical, emotional and mental), has improved significantly, when they are willing spending time both in the gym and outdoors. However, health represents more than physical exercises, well-being is equally necessary for the mental well-being of children. Nature increases positive emotions, reduces stress, frustration, and it is beneficial not only for overactive children.

"Plants communicate directly with our immune system and unconscious without us even needing to touch, much less swallow them. This fascinating interaction between human and plant is hugely significant for medicine and psychotherapy and is just starting to be understood by science. It keeps us physically and mentally healthy and prevents illness. In the future, contact with plants has to play an important role in treating physical illness and mental disorders" (Arvay, 2018).

But the reasons for seeking a "connection" with nature are numerous and not always inspired by health emergencies. It is obvious that the return to nature is related to the need to care for someone, which seems to be a factor in giving children a meaning in life. Of course, the goal is also important: the feeling of responsibility. Children are very sensitive when involved in the care of nature, which they understand as a common good, and whose conservation depends strictly on the responsibility of each one. But, mainly in the forest, they discover what biodiversity is and why it is so important, even from a human or cultural point of view. In addition, children learn that they are not detached from the rest of the world, but in a relationship of "dependence" with all other forms of life that populate the Earth.

An outdoor kindergarten is one of the best examples of applying education in direct contact with the rural world, where the child can learn about animals, the vegetable garden and everything the farm environment can offer. "Thus are presented examples of kindergartens housed in a farm, 'farm kindergartens,' and the story of the kindergartens in the forest is told; it is also suggested the possibility of bringing the rural environment into the classroom, and the classroom into the rural area, through new links between various social actors. In all the experiences told here, the main theme is the relationship with and through the environment: agricultural or natural, it is the place where it comes into contact with itself, with plants, with animals and with others and then together we will grow" (Durastanti et al., 2016).

Eco Farm Kindergartens is a place with no walls, no ceilings, where children can be outdoors, twirl in the grass and play with leaves and pieces of wood, but at the same time learn the fascinating mysteries of nature. These small kindergartens open in large agricultural areas, so in rural area, a simple, family environment in which the child plays outdoors with plants and animals and enjoys organic snacks. A natural environment, such as that of the farm, favors from an early age a "natural" relationship between the child and the environment and represents an unusual opportunity for the formation of healthy and responsible adults. However, I find it very important to point out that it was the Garden of Eden – Paradise, the place that man considered the first moment of its origin. The garden surrounded by the intoxicating fragrance of flowers should induce the child a behavioral transformation, through a clearer inner vision, which makes him understand the passing of time and the succession of seasons. Indeed, everyone should have a small piece of land that will be cultivated for their own existence. But, of course, we are aware that every child will adorn their little earthly paradise, with all kinds of vegetables, fruits and flowers.

Everyone who loves nature knows how gardening is the art of growing flowers, different fruits and plants, both for ornamental purposes and for food. It is now known, at least in part, that taking care of a small green space, or flowers and vegetables, has a beneficial effect on the child's health. If all this is true, we can understand how an active relationship (cutting the grass, moving the dirt or even caring for another living being), or being passive with nature (enjoying the beauty of the landscape), can promote natural therapeutic properties of green spaces. The vegetation has the capacity to reduce stress, favoring the recovery of the conditions of physiological balance: – neuro (brain) – psycho (emotions) – immunological (immune system). Not everything that surrounds us and supports us in life is necessarily therapeutic. A catalyst for healing and renewal is "only" the presence of flowers, fruits, bees, birds and other animals, harmonious songs and sounds, which remove any disorder from the soul.

L'Horticultural therapy, or more precisely the care of the garden, understood not as a simple therapy, but as an attitude of responsibility, has been working perfectly for years, and in thousands of cases, because people and plants have the same rhythms of life. Inspired by the Montessori principles, *help me do it myself*, the kindergarten staff constantly develops a whole series of so-called eco-therapy practices, such as tree therapy, play therapy, chromotherapy and music therapy. But probably one of the most popular alternative therapies in Europe is the *tree therapy*, which is part of the field of bio-natural disciplines, aimed at the well-being of the child. In fact, it has been found that the forest participates in the prevention and treatment of diseases, first and foremost, by the phytotherapeutic substances released by the trees. "Forest air is a rich biomedical mixture of substances that we can inhale or absorb through our skin, and plants release volatile compounds valad 'Terpenes' which significantly increase our immune functioning" (Arvay, 2018).

For example, the conifers emit volatile oils that stimulate the blood circulation, the birch trees, through their different aromas, stimulate the release of hormones as well as of the neuro-transmitters (noradrenaline, dopamine and vasopressin). Feelings, passions, emotions and behaviors are determined by the complex chemical reactions that take place in our brain, but also in the peripheral nervous system. Perhaps due importance is not given to the contribution of silvo therapy to the release or inhibition of certain neuro-transmitters. Thus, silvo therapy has an interesting future, including the curative process with the help of trees-shrubs and space-therapy-cure, using the perspective to obtain a harmonious spatial structure. A practice that obviously works only in a naturalistic context, which allows a broader discovery of the beauty of the forest, but not only: it also has therapeutic virtues.

In the particular case of children with attention disorders (ADHD), this method of healing can inhibit the manifestations of hyperactivity or impulsivity, stimulating concentration, intuition and clear ideas. In fact, the child has the sixth sense or instinct, a natural gift that allows him to interpret, in a powerful and clear way, the events that take place in the outside world. It should also be emphasized that nature offers children the means and opportunity to develop all their senses, such as to taste and smell the aromatic plants that surround them from all sides. "Children live through the senses. Sensory experiences connect the outer world to the inner, hidden and affective world. The natural environment is the main source of sensory stimulation and, therefore, the freedom to explore and play with it through the senses is essential for the inner life" (Oliverio & Oliverio Ferraris, 2011).

The benefits that can be obtained by doing physical activity, or by doing other activities, using generally green spaces, are of considerable importance and refer to the physical-motor, social, cognitive, affective and emotional development. In these spaces, which we can define as "green areas," the child must feel important to the others, or at least not so inferior, and must be able to enjoy a normal life. In the green areas, they are free to express their feelings, because the plants, like the animals, do not judge, do not directly impose their wishes and respect the inclinations and rhythm of the child.

Regardless if it is an agricultural landscape, either a forest or a pastoral one, these picturesque areas favor relaxation, stimulate physical activities in the open air, and at the same time, have a beneficial effect on the nervous system as well as on the immune and endocrine system. The activity carried out in nature is essential for the proper functioning of the different organs and internal systems, such as the arteries, the lungs and the heart, in fact, it is of fundamental importance in terms of metabolic processes. Nature is therefore a place that contributes to reducing anxiety and stress, facilitates interpersonal communication and teaches us to cultivate relationships of trust and honesty, improving the level and quality of our lives. To conclude, I think it is useful to mention Maria Montessori who pointed out the special connection between childhood and nature. Montessori wrote, first of all, to arouse in the mind and heart of the educator the interest towards nature, but also to determine an attitude more sensitive to the needs of the children, implicitly recognizing their value.

"When he knows that some animals have need of him, that the little plants will dry up if he does not water them, his love binds together with a new thread the passing moments and the day which is to follow. Watch the little ones as on one morning, after they had for many days, with loving care, placed food and water near the brooding doves, they discover the nestlings! Another day, it is a number of delightful chickens which are there, where before there had been the eggs which the hen had been keeping under her wings for so long. What tenderness and what immense enthusiasm! There is born in the children the desire to give further help; they collect little bits of straw, threads of old cotton material, wisps of cotton-wool, for the birds which are building their nests under the roof or on the trees in the garden. And a chorus of chirping, growing all round about, gives them thanks" (Montessori, 1948).

Chapter III

Development of children personality through the outdoor activities – research

III.1 Objectives of the research

The present study was designed by the researcher. The purpose of the study is to *determine whether the outdoor kindergartens provide a 5-year-old preschool child with a better learning environment in terms of developing their skills, compared to the traditional kindergarten-learning environment.*

In order to achieve the goal, the following specific objectives were formulated:

- **S.O.1:** Applying the Independent Learning Development Questionnaire (CHILD) (3–5) to collect data on 5-year-old preschoolers' skills, from 2 types of kindergartens: *outdoor kindergartens* and *traditional kindergartens;*
- **S.O.2:** Determine and compare the level of skill development of 5-year-preschool children in outdoor and traditional kindergartens for each of the following *4 skill categories:*
  - Emotional abilities;
  - Social skills;
  - Cognitive abilities;
  - Motivational skills;
- **S.O.3:** Establish the predictive value of the preschool children's gender over the degree of development of their emotional, social, cognitive and motivational abilities;
- **S.O.4:** Establishing the predictive value of the 5-year preschool children's learning environment, namely the type of kindergarten they participate in (outdoor or traditional) on the level of development of their emotional, social, cognitive and motivational abilities;

- **S.O.5:** Establishing correlations between the development of the four categories of abilities of preschool children (emotional, social, cognitive and motivational) for both outdoor and traditional kindergartens;
- **S.O.6:** Opening new horizons for further research on the learning environment in outdoor kindergartens, namely its role in the development of preschool children.

III.2 Research hypotheses

This research aims to verify the veracity of three general assumptions, each of which also has several specific hypotheses.

General hypothesis 1:

There are significant differences in the level of childhood skills development of 5-year-old children, depending on their gender.
Specific hypothesis:

1.1. The degree of development of the emotional abilities of 5-year-old preschool children significantly differs depending on their gender.

1.2. The degree of development of social skills of 5-year-old preschool children significantly differs depending on their gender.

1.3. The degree of cognitive development of 5-year-old preschool children significantly differs depending on their gender.

1.4. The degree of motivational skills' development of 5-year-old preschool children significantly differs depending on their gender.

General hypotheses 2:

There are significant differences in the level of skills development of 5-year-old preschool children, depending on their learning environment, and the kind of kindergarten they take part in.
Specific hypotheses:

2.1. The emotional abilities of 5-year-olds are significantly more developed in preschoolers in outdoor kindergartens compared to the preschools in traditional kindergartens.

2.2. The social abilities of 5-year-olds are significantly more developed in preschoolers in outdoor kindergartens compared to the preschools in traditional kindergartens.

2.3. The cognitive abilities of 5-year-olds are significantly more developed in preschoolers in outdoor kindergartens compared to the preschools in traditional kindergartens.

2.4. The motivational abilities of 5-year-olds are significantly more developed in preschoolers in outdoor kindergartens compared to the preschools in traditional kindergartens.

General hypothesis 3:

There are statistically significant positive relationships between different categories of abilities of 5-year-old preschoolers.

Specific hypotheses:

3.1. The emotional, social, cognitive and motivational abilities of pre-school children in outdoor kindergartens correlate positively.

3.2. The emotional, social, cognitive and motivational abilities of pre-school children in traditional kindergartens correlate positively.

III.3 Description of the method and the data collection tool

In order to achieve the proposed objectives and verify the research assumptions, we have chosen a *survey based on a questionnaire* as a method of data collection.

The main reason why we chose the questionnaire as a data collation tool is the specificity of this research, namely to compare the preschool children's skills in the traditional kindergartens with preschoolers in outdoor kindergartens. Given that there are no outdoor kindergartens in our country, or that they are newly established, with not enough children enrolled, it was necessary to question some subjects participating in such kindergartens from another country, the Czech Republic being elected.

Other *reasons behind choosing the questionnaire* are:

- It is economical and easy to apply, and can also be transmitted and filled in by email or on-line platforms;

- Closed questions provide a large amount of information that can be centralized in a short time;
- If submitted online, the questionnaire can easily be filled-in by subjects from different locations and countries;
- As research involves the investigation of a large number of subjects, this tool guarantees a secure and economic form of data acquisition.

In order to determine the development of the skills of preschool children aged 5 years, we chose the *Independent Learning Development Questionnaire (CHILD) 5*, a tool developed in 2009 by Professor PhD D. Whitebread at Cambridge University. Being elaborated in English, it was necessary to translate this tool into Romanian and Czech.

The questionnaire used includes *22 items*, with closed answers, for the assessment of preschool children's skills, aged five years old, as follows:

- Emotional skills – 5 items: *items1, 2, 3, 4 and 5*;
- Social skills – 5 items: *items 6, 7, 8, 9 and 10*;
- Cognitive skills – 7 items: *items 11, 12, 13, 14, 15, 16 and 17*;
- Motivational skills – 5 items: *items 18, 19, 20, 21 and 22*.

Each of the 22 items has been rated on a Likert scale from 1 to 4, where: *1 = never, 2 = sometimes, 3 = usually, and 4 = always*. The Likert scale was used as this is a simple, fast and efficient way of measuring assessments.

The only personal data requested for the respondents were *the preschoolers' gender, the age group of 5 years old, and the type of kindergarten they participate in* – outdoor or traditional.

The questionnaire was distributed between February and March 2016, as follows:

- In **Romania,** the questionnaire translated into Romanian was distributed to several *traditional kindergartens in Botosani County*. The distribution of the questionnaires was done through personal contact, as the researcher is a teacher in an important preschool education institution in this municipality. Respondents from Romania completed *54 questionnaires* in printed format, by ticking the chosen answers.
- In the **Czech Republic,** *several outdoor kindergartens in Prague and Ostrava*, both municipal and private, were randomly selected from the

Internet. The Czech-language questionnaire was sent by email in the form of an attachment to the directors of these outdoor kindergartens, together with an information letter presenting the importance of the study and making a clear reference to the confidentiality and anonymity of the data. Respondents from the Czech Republic completed 54 *questionnaires* in electronic format, sending them to the researcher by e-mail as an attachment.

The research tool used, translated into Romanian, can be found in *Annex A*.

III.4 Subjects of the research

The subjects of this research are *108 preschool children*, 5 years of age, of whom: 54 participate in *outdoor kindergartens in the Czech Republic*, in the cities of Prague and Ostrava and *54 in the traditional kindergartens in Romania*, Botosani County.

Since the 5-year old age group is a less appropriate study class for a reliable data collection, questionnaires were filled in by child educators who noted the gender of preschool, the type of kindergarten they were attending, and the appreciation of the 22 of the items, respectively the emotional, social, cognitive and motivational abilities of the children.

The distribution of the 108 5-year-old preschool children is shown in Tabs 1–2 and Figs 1–2.

Tab. 1 Distribution of 5-years-old preschool children by gender

	Children in outdoor kindergartens		Children in traditional kindergartens		All subjects	
	Frequency	Percent	Frequency	Percent	Frequency	Percent
Masculine	27	50,00 %	27	50,00 %	54	50,00 %
Feminine	27	50,00 %	27	50,00 %	54	50,00 %
Total	54	100,00 %	54	100,00 %	108	100,00 %

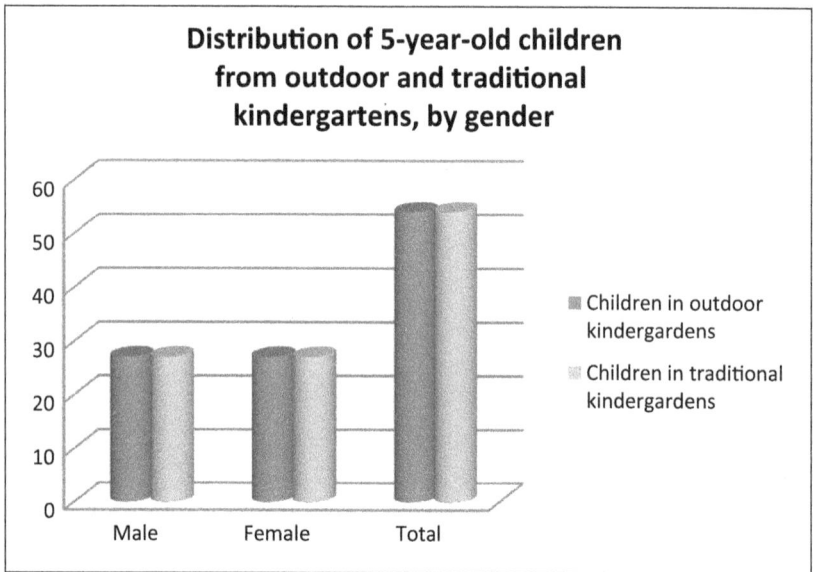

Distribution of 5-year-old children from outdoor and traditional kindergartens, by gender

Legend: Children in outdoor kindergardens; Children in traditional kindergardens

Fig. 1 Distribution of 5-year-old children, from outdoor and traditional kindergartens, by gender

Tab. 2 Distribution of 5-years-old children depending on the kind of kindergartens they attend

	Frequency	Percent
Outdoor kindergartens	54	50,00 %
Traditional kindergartens	54	50,00 %
Total	108	100,00 %

III.5 Coding, analysis and data-processing procedures

After establishing the objectives and research hypotheses, we have chosen the research tool that is most relevant to them, and to ascertain to the greatest extent possible, the veracity of the premises is formulated.

The CHILD 3–5 questionnaire described in the previous paragraph for assessing the abilities of 5-year-olds was completed by 54 teachers of preschools in kindergartens in the Czech Republic, in the cities of Prague and Ostrava, and by 54 preschool teachers from traditional kindergartens

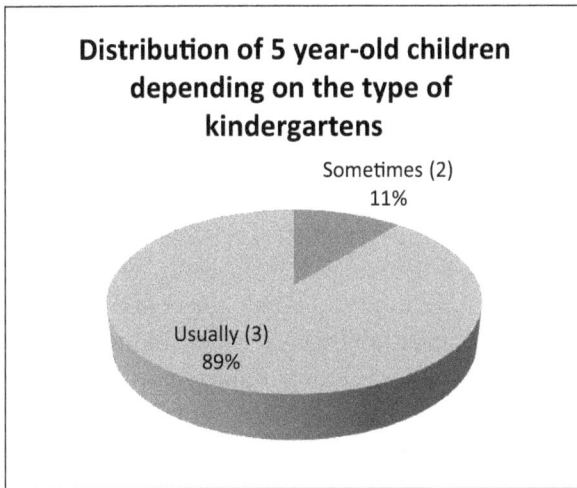

Fig. 2 Distribution of 5-year-old children depending on the type of kindergartens they attend

in Romania, from Botosani County. The completion of the questionnaire was done by ticking a single answer for each of the 22 items.

After data collection, it followed their insertion into SPSS (Statistical Package for Social Sciences), respectively, their *coding.*

Label variables (personal data) were encoded as follows:

⇨ *Gender of preschool children:*
1 = male, 2 = female;
⇨ *Type of kindergartens attended by preschool children:*
1= outdoor kindergartens, 2 = traditional kindergartens.

The 22 items of the questionnaire were coded with ordinal values from 1 to 4, as follows: *1 = Never, 2 = Sometimes, 3 = Usually, and 4 = Always.*

Using the "Compute variable" option, the *arithmetic averages* for each category of preschool children's abilities were calculated as follows:

• Average emotional abilities: (items 1 + 2 + 3 + 4 + 5) / 5;
• Average social skills: (items 6 + 7 + 8 + 9 + 10) / 5;
• Average cognitive abilities: (item 11 + 12 + 13 + 14 + 15 + 16 + 17) / 7;
• Average of motivational skills: (items 18 + 19 + 20 + 21 + 22) / 5.

From these averages there were some gross scores with values between 1,00 and 4,00, which were interpreted on the following *levels of the development of the respective abilities:*1 = weak development (for averages between 1.00 and 1.99), 2 = moderately developed (for averages between 2.00 and 2.99 and 3 = well developed (for averages between 3.00 and 4.00).

The *statistical analysis* consisted of the use of frequency tables and charts, T-tests for independent samples, and Pearson binary correlations to verify the validity of the research hypotheses. With the help of tables and frequency charts, the degree of development of the emotional, social, cognitive and motivational abilities of 5-year-old preschoolers in both outdoor kindergarten and traditional kindergartens was determined.

To *test the first research hypothesis*, respectively, to measure significant differences in the level of childhood skills development of 5-year-old children by gender, the *T-test for independent samples* was used to analyze significant differences between emotional, social, cognitive and motivational abilities of male and female preschoolers.

To *test the second research hypothesis*, respectively, to measure significant differences in the level of development of 5-year-old children's skills based on the learning environment, the *T-test for independent samples* for the analysis of some significant differences between the emotional, social, cognitive and motivational abilities of children in outdoor kindergartens and those in traditional kindergartens.

To *verify the third hypothesis of the research*, the *Pearson binary correlations* were used to analyze the existence of statistically significant positive relationships between:

• The emotional, social, cognitive and motivational abilities of preschool children in outdoor kindergartens;
• The emotional, social, cognitive and motivational abilities of preschool children in traditional kindergartens.

Finally, the data has been interpreted so that the final conclusions are as valid as possible.

III.6 Overall results

As detailed in this chapter, *data coding, analysis* and *processing procedures*, based on the assessments made in the 22 items, it has been determined the degree of development for each of the four categories of preschool children's abilities, aged 5 years.

III.6.1 Comparative analysis of the emotional abilities of children in outdoor and traditional kindergartens

Tabs 3–8 present the appreciation of outdoor and traditional kindergarten teachers about the emotional abilities of the preschoolers they educate (items 1–5) and the degree of development of these skills.

In Tab. 3, it shows that the number of children who answered that they understand the consequences of their own behavior is higher for the children who are learning in the outdoor kindergarten. In traditional kindergarten they choose sometime and usually (89 %) for understanding the consequences and others children answer usually and always (81 %).

Tab. 3 Frequency for item, "'Understand and talk about the consequences of his or her behavior and of others"

	Children in outdoor kindergartens		Children in traditional kindergartens		All children	
	Frequency	Percent	Frequency	Percent	Frequency	Percent
Sometimes (2)	10	18,52 %	23	42,59 %	33	30,56 %
Usually (3)	31	57,41 %	25	46,3 %	56	51,85 %
Always (4)	13	24,07 %	6	11,11 %	19	17,59 %
Total	54	100,00 %	54	100,00 %	108	100,00 %

Tab. 4 Answers for item 2, "Assign new tasks with trust"

	Children in outdoor kindergartens		Children in traditional kindergartens		All children	
	Frequency	Percent	Frequency	Percent	Frequency	Percent
Sometimes (2)	4	7,41 %	14	25,93 %	18	16,67 %
Usually (3)	23	42,59 %	26	48,15 %	49	45,37 %
Always (4)	27	50,00 %	14	25,93 %	41	37,96 %
Total	54	100,00 %	54	100,00 %	108	100,00 %

Development of children personality

For this question, children who learn in outdoor activities perceived that always (50 %) they assign new issues with trust, but for children who attend traditional kindergarten they choose usually as most frequent answer (48 %).

For this item was not very different for the both category of children and for they are possible to evaluate and monitor own results and to keep properly.

Tab. 5 Assessments for item 3, "Concentrated and resistant to distraction"

	Children in outdoor kindergartens		Children in traditional kindergartens		All children	
	Frequency	Percent	Frequency	Percent	Frequency	Percent
Sometimes (2)	2	3,70 %	10	18,52 %	12	11,11 %
Usually (3)	22	40,74 %	33	61,11 %	55	50,93 %
Always (4)	30	55,56 %	11	20,37 %	41	37,96 %
Total	54	100,00 %	54	100,00 %	108	100,00 %

Tab. 6 Answers for item 4, "Monitor your progress and seek help properly"

	Children in outdoor kindergartens		Children in traditional kindergartens		All children	
	Frequency	Percent	Frequency	Percent	Frequency	Percent
Sometimes (2)	2	3,70 %	9	16,67 %	11	10,19 %
Usually (3)	29	53,70 %	27	50,00 %	56	51,85 %
Always (4)	23	42,59 %	18	33,33 %	41	37,96 %
Total	54	100,00 %	54	100,00 %	108	100,00 %

Tab. 7 Assessments for item 5, "Resilient to difficulties"

	Children in outdoor kindergartens		Children in traditional kindergartens		All children	
	Frequency	Percent	Frequency	Percent	Frequency	Percent
Sometimes (2)	1	1,85 %	7	12,96 %	8	7,41 %
Usually (3)	28	51,85 %	36	66,67 %	64	59,26 %
Always (4)	25	46,30 %	11	20,37 %	36	33,33 %
Total	54	100,00 %	54	100,00 %	108	100,00 %

Tab. 8 Degree of development of emotional abilities of preschool children

	Children in outdoor kindergartens		Children in traditional kindergartens		All children	
	Frequency	Percent	Frequency	Percent	Frequency	Percent
Moderately developed	1	1,85 %	17	31,48 %	18	16,67 %
Well developed	53	98,15 %	37	68,52 %	90	83,33 %
Total	54	100,00 %	54	100,00 %	108	100,00 %

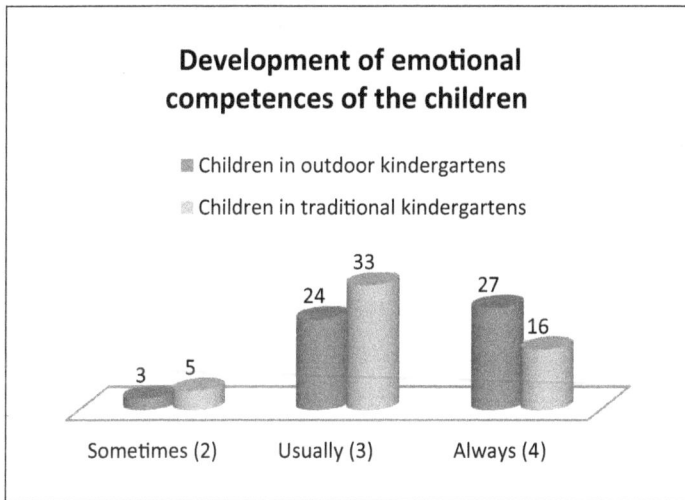

Development of emotional competences of the children

▩ Children in outdoor kindergartens

▩ Children in traditional kindergartens

3 5   24 33   27 16

Sometimes (2)   Usually (3)   Always (4)

Fig. 3 Comparative analysis of the degree of development of emotional abilities between children in outdoor kindergartens and those in traditional kindergartens

The comparative analysis of the degree of development of emotional abilities between preschool children in outdoor kindergartens and those in traditional kindergartens is shown in Figs 3 and 4 shows the distribution of the degree of development of emotional abilities for all preschool children, subjects of this research.

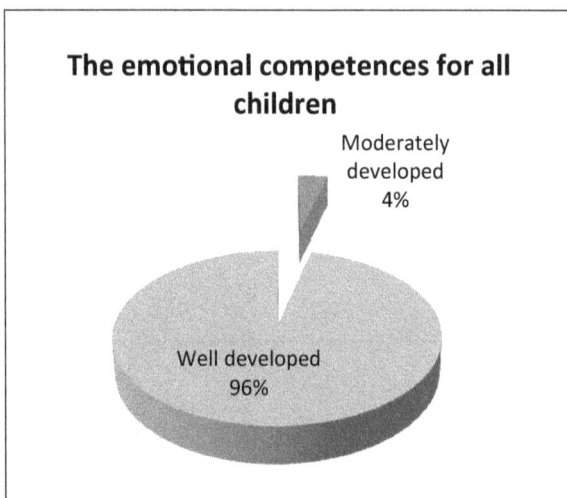

Fig. 4 The degree of development of the emotional abilities of all children

III.6.2 Comparative analysis of the social abilities of preschool children in outdoor kindergartens and traditional kindergartens

Tabs 9–14 render the appreciation of kindergarten teachers and traditional teachers about the social skills of preschoolers they educate (items 6–10) and the degree of development of these skills.

Tab. 9 Appraisals for item 6, "Negotiate when and how to fulfill a responsibility"

	Children in outdoor kindergartens		Children in traditional kindergartens		All children	
	Frequency	Percent	Frequency	Percent	Frequency	Percent
Never (1)	1	1,85 %	1	1,85 %	2	1,85 %
Sometimes (2)	16	29,63 %	23	42,59 %	39	36,11 %
Usually (3)	25	46,30 %	22	40,74 %	48	44,44 %
Always (4)	12	22,22 %	8	14,81 %	19	17,59 %
Total	54	100,00 %	54	100,00 %	108	100,00 %

Tab. 10 Assessments for item 7, "Can solve their social issues with colleagues alone"

	Children in outdoor kindergartens		Children in traditional kindergartens		All children	
	Frequency	Percent	Frequency	Percent	Frequency	Percent
Sometimes (2)	3	5,56 %	20	37,04 %	23	21,30 %
Usually (3)	27	50,00 %	23	42,59 %	49	45,37 %
Always (4)	24	44,44 %	11	20,37 %	36	33,33 %
Total	54	100,00 %	54	100,00 %	108	100,00 %

Tab. 11 Assessments for item 8, "Learned to be patient and to share things independently"

	Children in outdoor kindergartens		Children in traditional kindergartens		All children	
	Frequency	Percent	Frequency	Percent	Frequency	Percent
Sometimes (2)	3	5,56 %	11	20,37 %	14	12,96 %
Usually (3)	28	51,85 %	31	57,41 %	59	54,63 %
Always (4)	23	42,59 %	12	22,22 %	35	32,41 %
Total	54	100,00 %	54	100,00 %	108	100,00 %

Tab. 12 Assessments for item 9, "Engage in cooperative activities with colleagues independently"

	Children in outdoor kindergarten		Children in traditional kindergartens		All children	
	Frequency	Percent	Frequency	Percent	Frequency	Percent
Sometimes (2)	3	5,56 %	6	11,11 %	9	8,33 %
Usually (3)	24	44,44 %	39	72,22 %	64	59,26 %
Always (4)	27	50,00 %	9	16,67 %	35	32,41 %
Total	54	100,00 %	54	100,00 %	108	100,00 %

The comparative analysis of the degree of development of social abilities between preschool children in outdoor kindergartens and in traditional kindergartens is shown in Fig. 6. Fig. 7 shows the distribution of the social skills development degree for all preschool children, subjects of this research.

Tab. 13 Assessments for item 10, "Is aware of others' feelings helps them feel comfortable"

	Children in outdoor kindergartens		Children in traditional kindergartens		All children	
	Frequency	Percent	Frequency	Percent	Frequency	Percent
Sometimes (2)	3	5,56 %	5	9,26 %	8	7,41 %
Usually (3)	24	44,44 %	33	61,11 %	57	52,78 %
Always (4)	27	50,00 %	16	29,63 %	43	39,81 %
Total	54	100,00 %	54	100,00 %	108	100,00 %

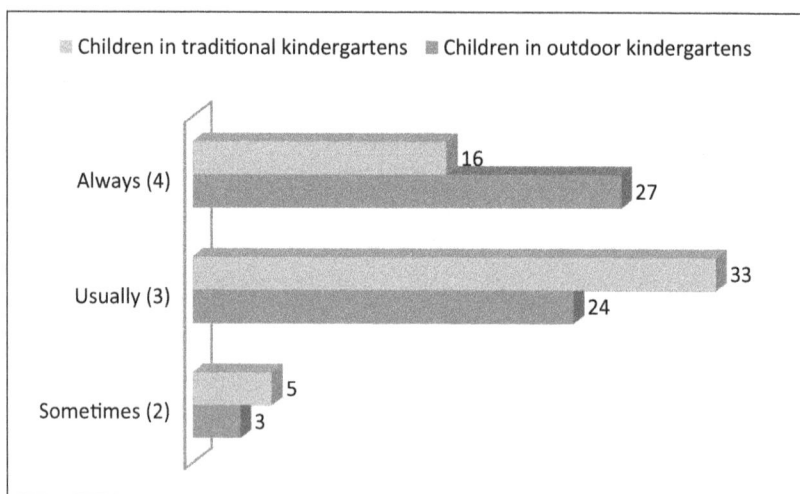

Fig. 5 Answer for item: Is aware of others' feelings helps them feel comfortable

III.6.3 Comparative analysis of the cognitive abilities of preschool children in outdoor and traditional kindergartens

Tabs 15–22 render the teachers' feedback in outdoor and traditional kindergartens on the cognitive abilities of preschoolers they are educating (items 11–17) and the degree of development of these abilities.

The comparative analysis of the degree of development of cognitive abilities between preschool children in outdoor and traditional kindergartens

Tab. 14 The level of development of the social abilities of children

	Children in outdoor kindergartens		Children in traditional kindergartens		All children	
	Frequency	Percent	Frequency	Percent	Frequency	Percent
Moderately developed	2	3,70 %	22	40,74 %	24	22,22 %
Well developed	52	96,30 %	32	59,26 %	84	77,78 %
Total	54	100,00 %	54	100,00 %	108	100,00 %

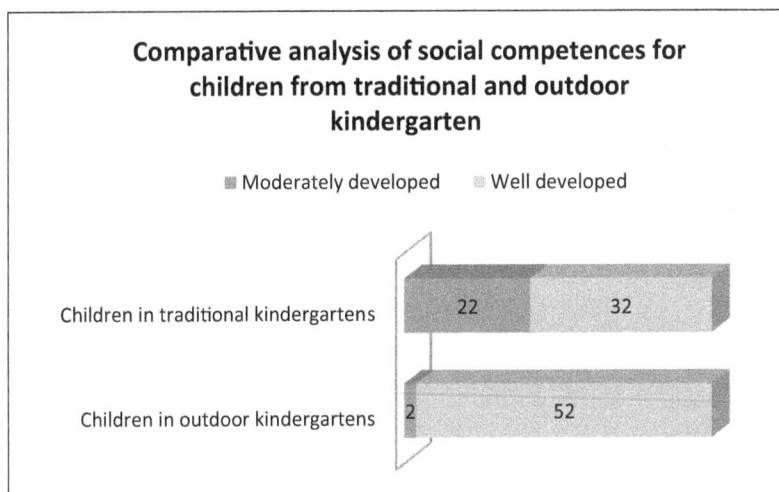

Fig. 6 Comparative analysis of the degree of development of social skills among preschool children in outdoor and traditional kindergartens

is shown in Fig. 8. Fig. 9 shows the distribution of cognitive skills development for all preschool children, subjects of this research.

III.6.4 Comparative analysis of the motivational abilities of preschoolers in outdoor and traditional kindergartens

Tabs 23–28 render the appreciation of teacher in outdoor and traditional kindergartens about the skills of the preschoolers they are educating (items 18–22) and the degree of development of these skills.

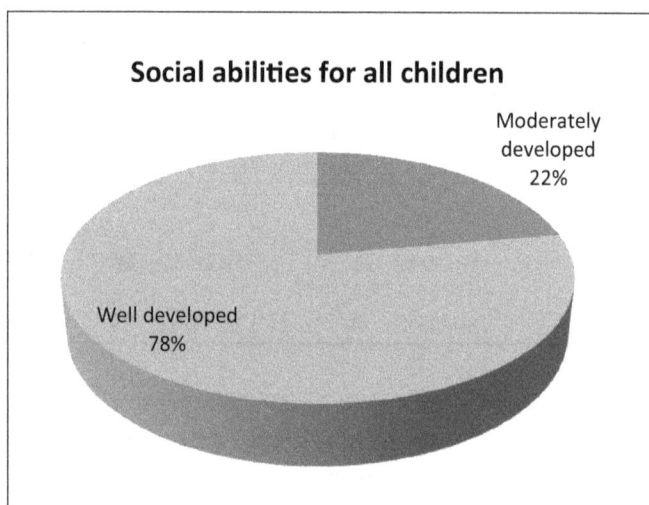

Fig. 7 The degree of development of the social abilities of all children

Tab. 15 Assessments for item 11, "Is aware of its strengths and weaknesses"

	Children in outdoor kindergartens		Children in traditional kindergartens		All children	
	Frequency	Percent	Frequency	Percent	Frequency	Percent
Sometimes (2)	5	9,26 %	18	33,33 %	23	21,30 %
Usually (3)	30	55,56 %	30	55,56 %	60	55,56 %
Always (4)	19	35,19 %	6	11,11 %	25	23,15 %
Total	54	100,00 %	54	100,00 %	108	100,00 %

Tab. 16 Assessments for item 12, "May communicate about what he did or learned"

	Children in outdoor kindergartens		Children in traditional kindergartens		All children	
	Frequency	Percent	Frequency	Percent	Frequency	Percent
Sometimes (2)	3	5,56 %	9	16,67 %	12	11,11 %
Usually (3)	26	48,15 %	33	61,11 %	59	54,63 %
Always (4)	25	46,30 %	12	22,22 %	37	34,26 %
Total	54	100,00 %	54	100,00 %	108	100,00 %

Tab. 17 Assessments for item 13 "Can talk about future activities planned"

	Children in outdoor kindergartens		Children in traditional kindergartens		All children	
	Frequency	Percent	Frequency	Percent	Frequency	Percent
Sometimes (2)	5	9,26 %	12	22,22 %	17	15,74 %
Usually (3)	27	50,00 %	27	50,00 %	54	50,00 %
Always (4)	22	40,74 %	15	27,78 %	37	34,26 %
Total	54	100,00 %	54	100,00 %	108	100,00 %

Tab. 18 Assessments for item 14, "Can make choices and informed decisions"

	Children in outdoor kindergartens		Children in traditional kindergartens		All children	
	Frequency	Percent	Frequency	Percent	Frequency	Percent
Sometimes (2)	4	7,41 %	6	11,11 %	10	9,26 %
Usually (3)	29	53,7 %	27	50,00 %	56	51,85 %
Always (4)	21	38,89 %	21	38,89 %	42	38,89 %
Total	54	100,00 %	54	100,00 %	108	100,00 %

Tab. 19 Assessments for item 15, "Ask questions and suggest answers"

	Children in outdoor kindergartens		Children in traditional kindergartens		All children	
	Frequency	Percent	Frequency	Percent	Frequency	Percent
Sometimes (2)	5	9,26 %	5	9,26 %	10	9,26 %
Usually (3)	29	53,70 %	32	59,26 %	61	56,48 %
Always (4)	20	37,04 %	17	31,48 %	37	34,26 %
Total	54	100,00 %	54	100,00 %	108	100,00 %

The comparative analysis of the degree of development of motivational skills between preschool children in outdoor and traditional kindergartens is shown in Fig. 10. Fig. 11 shows the distribution of the degree of development of motivational skills for all preschool children, subjects of this research.

Tab. 20 Assessments for item 16, "Use previously taught learning strategies"

	Children in outdoor kindergartens		Children in traditional kindergartens		All children	
	Frequency	Percent	Frequency	Percent	Frequency	Percent
Sometimes (2)	2	3,70 %	3	5,56 %	5	4,63 %
Usually (3)	33	61,11 %	36	66,67 %	69	63,89 %
Always (4)	19	35,19 %	15	27,78 %	34	31,48 %
Total	54	100,00 %	54	100,00 %	108	100,00 %

Tab. 21 Assessments for item 17, "Adopt previously heard language for own purposes"

	Children in outdoor kindergartens		Children in traditional kindergartens		All children	
	Frequency	Percent	Frequency	Percent	Frequency	Percent
Sometimes (2)	3	5,56 %	5	9,26 %	8	7,41 %
Usually (3)	23	42,59 %	33	61,11 %	56	51,85 %
Always (4)	28	51,85 %	16	29,63 %	44	40,74 %
Total	54	100,00 %	54	100,00 %	108	100,00 %

Tab. 22 Degree of development of cognitive abilities of children

	Children in outdoor kindergartens		Children in traditional kindergartens		All children	
	Frequency	Percent	Frequency	Percent	Frequency	Percent
Moderately developed	1	1,85 %	8	14,81 %	9	8,33 %
Well developed	53	98,15 %	46	85,19 %	99	91,67 %
Total	54	100,00 %	54	100,00 %	108	100,00 %

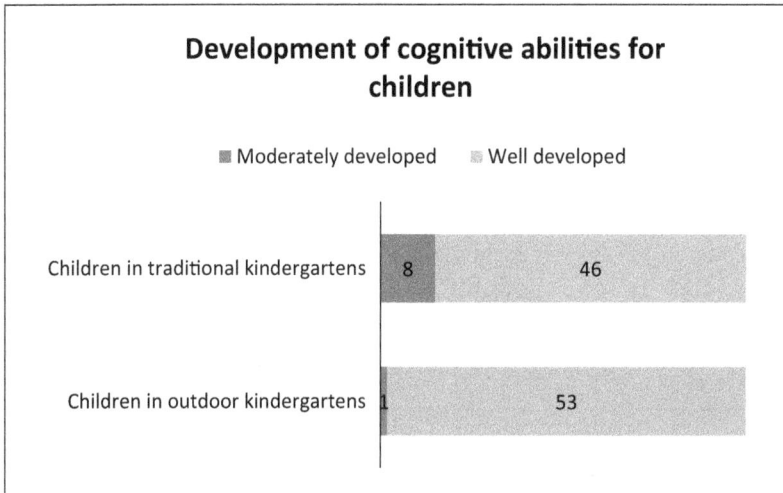

Fig. 8 Comparative analysis of the degree of development of cognitive abilities between preschool children in outdoor and traditional kindergartens

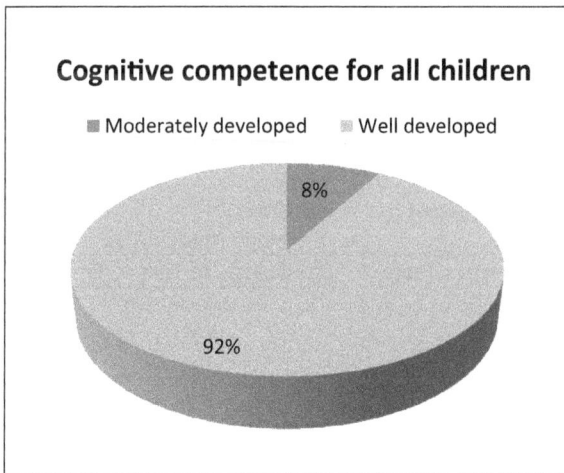

Fig. 9 The degree of development of the cognitive competence of all children

Tab. 23 Assessments for item 18, "Finds own resources without the help of adults"

	Children in outdoor kindergartens		Children in traditional kindergartens		All children	
	Frequency	Percent	Frequency	Percent	Frequency	Percent
Sometimes (2)	6	11,11 %	17	31,48 %	23	21,30 %
Usually (3)	27	50,00 %	29	53,70 %	56	51,85 %
Always (4)	21	38,89 %	8	14,81 %	29	26,85 %
Total	54	100,00 %	54	100,00 %	108	100,00 %

Tab. 24 Assessments for item 19, "Develops own ways to carry out tasks"

	Children in outdoor kindergartens		Children in traditional kindergartens		All children	
	Frequency	Percent	Frequency	Percent	Frequency	Percent
Sometimes (2)	2	3,70 %	8	14,81 %	10	9,26 %
Usually (3)	29	53,70 %	28	51,85 %	57	52,78 %
Always (4)	23	42,59 %	18	33,33 %	41	37,96 %
Total	54	100,00 %	54	100,00 %	108	100,00 %

Tab. 25 Assessments for item 20, "Initiates activities"

	Children in outdoor kindergartens		Children in traditional kindergartens		All children	
	Frequency	Percent	Frequency	Percent	Frequency	Percent
Sometimes (2)	4	7,41 %	4	7,41 %	8	7,41 %
Usually (3)	24	44,44 %	38	70,37 %	62	57,41 %
Always (4)	26	48,15 %	12	22,22 %	38	35,19 %
Total	54	100,00 %	54	100,00 %	108	100,00 %

III.7 Interpretation of research hypotheses

III.7.1 General hypothesis 1

There are significant differences in the level of childhood skills development of 5-year-old children, depending on their gender.

Tab. 26 Assessments for item 21, "Planning own tasks, purpose and objectives"

	Children in outdoor kindergartens		Children in traditional kindergartens		All children	
	Frequency	Percent	Frequency	Percent	Frequency	Percent
Sometimes (2)	2	3,70 %	7	12,96 %	9	8,33 %
Usually (3)	26	48,15 %	38	70,37 %	64	59,26 %
Always (4)	26	48,15 %	9	16,67 %	35	32,41 %
Total	54	100,00 %	54	100,00 %	108	100,00 %

Tab. 27 Assessments for item 22, "Enjoys solving problems"

	Children in outdoor kindergartens		Children in traditional kindergartens		All children	
	Frequency	Percent	Frequency	Percent	Frequency	Percent
Sometimes (2)	4	7,41 %	6	11,11 %	10	9,26 %
Usually (3)	19	35,19 %	27	50,00 %	46	42,59 %
Always (4)	31	57,41 %	21	38,89 %	52	48,15 %
Total	54	100,00 %	54	100,00 %	108	100,00 %

Tab. 28 Degree of development of the motivational abilities of preschool children

	Children in outdoor kindergartens		Children in traditional kindergartens		All children	
	Frequency	Percent	Frequency	Percent	Frequency	Percent
Moderately developed	1	1,85 %	8	14,81 %	9	8,33 %
Well developed	53	98,15 %	46	85,19 %	99	91,67 %
Total	54	100,00 %	54	100,00 %	108	100,00 %

This hypothesis refers to the degree of development of 5-year-old males' abilities compared to females. In terms of 4 categories of abilities, namely emotional, social, cognitive and motivational abilities, we divided this general hypothesis into 4 specific hypotheses. The four specific hypotheses refer to one category of abilities, according to which we assumed

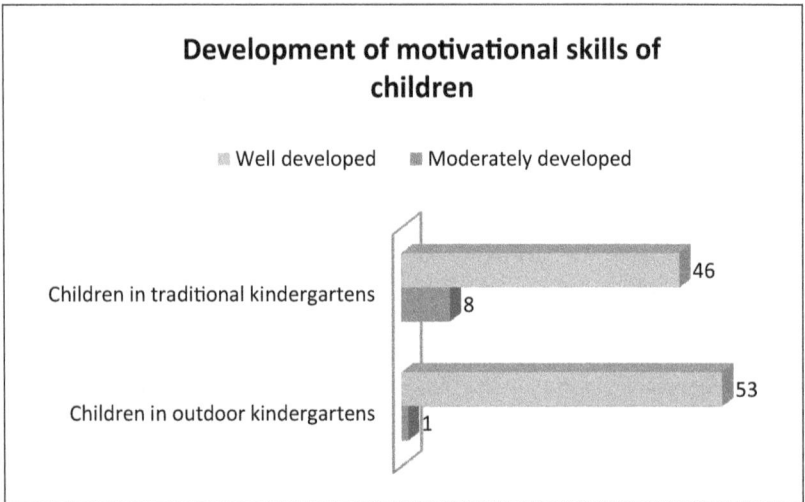

Fig. 10 Comparative analysis of the degree of development of motivational skills between children in outdoor and traditional kindergartens

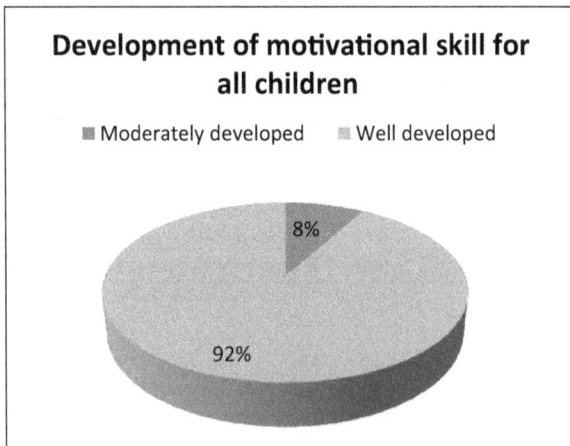

Fig. 11 The degree of development of the motivational abilities of all children

Tab. 29 Comparison of emotional abilities of preschool children by gender

	t	Sig. 2-tailed	Media M (N=54)	F (N=54)
Assesments for item 1 'Understand and talk about the consequences of his or her behavior and others'	2,29	0.024	2,72	3,02
Assesments for item 2, 'Approaches new tasks with confidence'	1,22	0.225	3,13	3,30
Assesments for item 3 'Focused and resisting distraction'	0,44	0.659	3,24	3,30
Assesments for item 4 'Monitors the progress and seeks help accordingly'	1,21	0.230	3,20	3,35
Assesments for item 5 'Persistent in the face of difficulties'	3,07	0.003	3,09	3,43
The degree of development of EMOTIONAL ABILITIES	1,55	0.124	2,78	2,89

Legend: t = value of t; sig. (2-tailed) = the 5 % level of significance of t (confidence interval is of 95 %).

that there will be significant differences in their degree of development, depending on the gender of children.

III.7.1.1 Specific hypothesis 1.1

The degree of development of the *emotional abilities* of 5-year-old pre-school children significantly differs according to their *gender.*

In order to verify this hypothesis, the t test for independent samples was used to *measure the existence of significant differences in the emotional abilities of 5-year-olds* (with reference both to the assessments for items 1–5 of the questionnaire, and to the underlying factor, respectively, the degree of development of emotional abilities) between male (N = 54) and female (N = 54) children. The values, the significant thresholds of t, as well as the appreciation environments of preschoolers in the two subgroups are shown in Tab. 29.

For differences to be considered significant, the significance level of t (2-tailed) must be less than 0.05. The lower the significance level, the more significant the differences between subgroups are.

Analyzing the data in Tab. 29 above, we find that although the *degree of development of the emotional abilities* of 5-year-old male and female preschoolers significantly differs statistically, the differences appear in the case of the assessments of 2 of the 5 items that make up this emotional factor, respectively items 1 and 5 of the questionnaire.

The average of assessments for *item 1* is significantly higher (t = 2.29, p. <0.05) for female preschool children compared to males. On average, 5-year-old female preschool children understand and can talk about the consequences of their behavior to others more frequently than 5-year-old male preschoolers.

The average of assessments for item 5 is significantly higher (t = 3.07, p <0.01) for female preschool children compared to males. On average, 5-year-old female preschoolers are more persistent in the face of more frequent difficulties than 5-year-old male preschoolers.

Considering the data analyzed, we can partially confirm the specific hypothesis 1.1, in the sense that, *although overall, emotional skills do not differ significantly between preschool girls and boys*, there are *significant gender differences only in relation to certain emotional components linked to the behavioral consequences and perseverance in the face of difficulties*, components that are *more developed for girls*.

III.7.1.2 Specific hypothesis 1.2

The degree of development of social skills of 5-year-old preschool children significantly differs depending on their gender.

In order to verify this hypothesis, the t test for independent samples was used to measure the existence of significant differences in the social skills of 5-year-old preschoolers (with reference both to the assessments for items 6–10 of the questionnaire and to the underlying factor, respectively, the degree of development of social abilities) between male (N = 54) and female (N = 54) children. The values, significance thresholds of t, as well as the appreciation environments of preschoolers in the two subgroups are shown in Tab. 30.

For differences to be considered significant, the significance level of t (2-tailed) must be less than 0.05. The lower the significance level, the differences between subgroups are more significant.

Tab. 30 Comparison of the social abilities of preschool children by gender

	t	Sig. 2-tailed	Media M (N=54)	F (N=54)
Assessments for item 6 *'Negotiates when and how to fulfill a responsibility'*	2,63	0.010	2,59	2,96
Assessments for Item 7, *'Can solve social issues with colleagues by himself'*	3,14	0.002	2,91	3,33
Assessments for item 8 *'Taught to be patient and to share things independently'*	1,65	0.103	3,09	3,30
Assessments for item 9, *'Engages in cooperative activities with colleagues independently'*	1,63	0.105	3,15	3,33
Assessments for item 10 *'Is aware that others' feelings helps them feel comfortable'*	3,12	0.002	3,15	3,50
The degree of development of SOCIAL ABILITIES	3,38	0.001	2,65	2,91

Legend: t = value of t; sig. (2-tailed) = significance level of 5 % of t (confidence interval is 95 %)

Analyzing the data in the Tab. 30 above, we find that there are *significant differences* between male and female preschoolers, both in terms of the *degree of development of their social skills* and as regards *the assessments of 3 of the 5 items* which make up this social factor.

Regarding the components of the social factor, we can see that there are significant differences depending on children's gender in the case of items 6, 7 and 10.

The average rating for *item 6* is significantly higher (t = 3.14, p <0.01) for female preschool children compared to males. On average, 5-year-old female preschoolers negotiate when and how to fulfill a responsibility much more frequent than 5-year-old male preschoolers.

The average rating for *item 7* is significantly higher (t = 3.07, p <0.01) for female preschool children compared to males. On average, 5-year-old female preschoolers can solve their social problems with their colleagues much more frequently than 5-year-old male preschoolers.

The average rating for *item 10* is significantly higher (t = 3.12, p. <0.01) for female preschool children compared to males. On average, 5-year-old

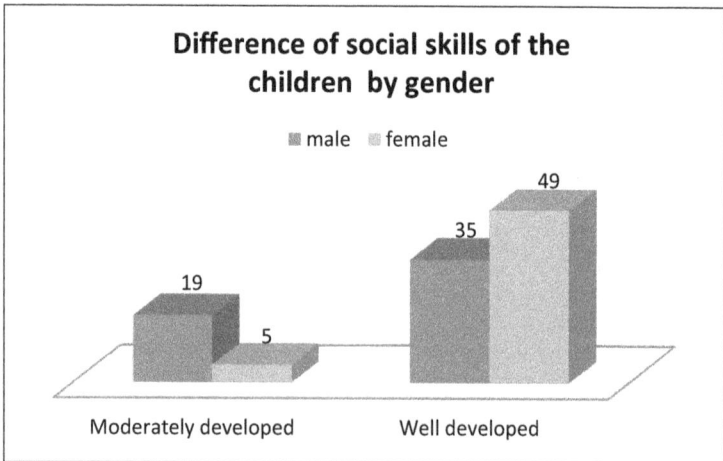

Fig. 12 Significant differences between male and female preschoolers in the degree of development of their social skills

female preschool children are aware of other people's feelings and help them feel more comfortable than most 5-year-old male preschoolers.

Regarding the significant differences in the development of social skills of male and female preschoolers, they are shown in the Fig. 12:

The social abilities of children are significantly better developed ($t = 3.38$, p. <0.01) for female preschool children compared to males.

As a conclusion, given that the *social skills* of male and female preschoolers significantly differs, both overall (as a factor) and at the level of *negotiation-related components, solving social issues and empathy*, we can confirm the specific hypothesis 1.2. In addition, the data analyzed allows us to say that these components and social skills are *much more developed for girls* than for boys, on these ages.

III.7.1.3 Specific hypothesis 1.3

The degree of *cognitive development* of 5-year-old children differs significantly depending on their genre.

In order to verify this hypothesis, the t test for independent samples was used to *measure the existence of significant differences in the cognitive abilities of 5-year-old preschoolers* (with reference both to the

Tab. 31 Comparison of cognitive abilities of preschool children by gender

	t	Sig. 2-tailed	Media M (N=54)	F (N=54)
Assessments for item 11,'*Is aware of its own strengths and weaknesses*'	0,29	0.775	3,00	3,04
Assessments for Item 12, '*Can communicate about what he or she did or learned*'	0,15	0.880	3,24	3,22
Assessments for item 13 '*Can talk about future planned activities*'	0,79	0.577	3,15	3,22
Assessments for item 14 '*Can make choices and make motivated decisions*'	0,92	0.362	3,24	3,35
Assessments for item 15 '*Asks questions and suggests answers*'	0,16	0.876	3,26	3,24
Assessments for item 16, '*Uses learning strategies previously taught*'	0,53	0.595	3,30	3,24
Assessments for item 17, '*Adopts previously heard language for own purposes*'	0,63	0.532	3,30	3,37
The degree of development of COGNITIVE ABILITIES	0,35	0.731	2,91	2,93

Legend: t = value of t; sig. (2-tailed) = significance level of 5 % of t (confidence interval is 95 %)

assessments for items 11–17 of the questionnaire, and to the underlying factor, respectively, the degree of development of cognitive abilities) between male (N = 54) and female (N = 54) children. The values, significance thresholds of t, as well as the appreciation environments of preschoolers in the two subgroups are shown in Tab. 31.

For differences to be considered significant, the significance level of t (2-tailed) must be less than 0.05. The lower the significance level, the more significant the differences between subgroups are.

Analyzing the data from Tab. 31, we find that between the two subgroups, male and female preschoolers, there are no significant differences in the degree of development of their cognitive abilities, nor in the assessments of those 7 elements of this cognitive factor, which leads to the *refutation of the specific hypothesis 1.3*.

Tab. 32 Comparison of the motivational abilities of preschool children by gender

	t	Sig. 2-tailed	Media M (N=54)	F (N=54)
Assessments for item 18 'Finds its own resources without the help of adults'	1,11	0.270	2,98	3,13
Assessments for item 19 'Develops own ways to perform tasks'	1,39	0.168	3,20	3,37
Assessments for item 20, 'Initiates Activities'	0,97	0.333	3,22	3,33
Assessments for Item 21, 'Planning own tasks, purpose and objectives'	0,00	1.00	3,24	3,24
Assessments for item 22, 'Enjoys solving problems'	2,73	0.007	3,22	3,56
The degree of development of MOTIVATIONAL ABILITIES	1,04	0.301	2,89	2,94

Legend: t = value of t; sig. (2-tailed) = significance level of 5 % of t (confidence interval is 95 %)

III.7.1.4 Specific hypothesis 1.4

The degree of development of *motivational abilities* of 5-year-old pre-school children significantly differs according to their *genre*.

In order to verify this hypothesis, the t test for independent samples was used to *measure the existence of significant differences in the motivational skills of 5-year-olds* (with reference both to the assessments for items 18–22 of the questionnaire and to the factor on the basis of these, respectively, the degree of development of motivational skills) between male (N = 54) and female (N = 54) children. The values, significance thresholds of t, as well as the appreciation environments of preschoolers in the two subgroups are shown in Tab. 32.

For differences to be considered significant, the significance level of t (2-tailed) must be less than 0.05. The lower the significance level, the more significant the differences between subgroups are.

Analyzing the data from Tab. 32 above, we find that although the degree of development of the motivational skills of 5-year-old male and female preschoolers differs statistically, the differences appear in the assessments for 1 of the 5 items that make up this motivational factor, respectively, item 22 of the questionnaire.

The average assessments for item 22 is significantly higher (t = 2.73, p. <0.01) for female preschool children compared to males. On average, 3–5-year-old female preschoolers enjoy problem-solving more frequent than 5-year-old male preschoolers.

Considering the data analyzed, we can partially confirm the specific hypothesis 1.4, in the sense that, *while overall, motivational skills do not differ significantly between preschool girls and boys*, there are *significant gender differences only in relation to a motivational component by the enthusiasm of problem-solving*, a *more developed component for girls*.

All the data analyzed in the specific hypotheses 1.1, 1.2, 1.3 and 1.4 lead to the *partial confirmation of the general hypothesis 1*, attesting to the fact that *there are significant differences only in the development of social skills of preschool children of 5 years depending on their genre*, these abilities being *much more developed for girls*.

However, *significant gender differences* also exist at the level of the assessment of certain *items* of the questionnaire, components of emotional, social and motivational factors as follows:

- *The emotional components related to behavioral consequences (item 1) and persistence to difficulties* (item 5) *are much more developed in the case of female preschoolers* compared to male preschoolers;
- *Social components related to bargaining* (item 6), *solving social problems* (item 7) *and empathy* (item 10) *are much more developed in the case of female preschoolers* compared to male preschoolers;
- *The motivational component related to the enthusiasm of problem-solving* (item 22) *is much more developed in the case of female preschoolers* compared to male preschoolers.

III.7.2 General hypothesis 2

There are significant differences in the level of childhood skills development of 5-year-old children, depending on their learning environment, and the kind of kindergarten they take part in.

This hypothesis refers to the development of abilities of 5-year-old pre-school children in outdoor kindergartens (in the Czech Republic), compared to those in traditional kindergartens (in Romania). In terms of

4 categories of abilities, respectively, emotional, social, cognitive and motivational abilities, we divided this general hypothesis into 4 specific hypotheses. The four specific hypotheses refer to one category of abilities, according to which we assumed that there will be significant differences in their degree of development, depending on the type of kindergartens attended by preschool children.

III.7.2.1 Specific hypothesis 2.1

The emotional abilities of 5-year-olds are *significantly more developed in preschools in outdoor kindergartens* compared to preschoolers in traditional kindergartens.

In order to verify this hypothesis, the t test for independent samples was used *to measure whether the emotional abilities of 5-year-old preschoolers* (with reference both to the assessments for items 1–5 of the questionnaire and to the factor determined on their basis, the level of development of emotional abilities) *are more statistically significantly developed* for children attending outdoor kindergartens (N = 54) compared to children attending traditional kindergartens (N = 54). The values, significance thresholds of t, as well as the appreciation environments of preschoolers in the two subgroups are shown in Tab. 33.

For differences to be considered significant, the significance level of t (2-tailed) must be less than 0.05. The lower the significance level, the more significant the differences between subgroups are.

Analyzing the data in Tab. 33, we find that there are *significant differences* between preschoolers in outdoor and traditional kindergartens, both in terms of the development of their emotional abilities and as regards the assessments of 4 out of 5 items that make up this emotional factor.

Concerning the *components* of the emotional factor, we can see that there are significant differences depending on the type of kindergartens in which children participate in items 1, 2, 3 and 5.

The average assessments for *item 1* are significantly higher (t = 2.91, p. <0.01) for preschool children in outdoor kindergartens compared to traditional kindergartens. On average, 5-year-old preschool children participating in outdoor kindergartens understand and can talk about the consequences of their own behavior more often than with 5-year-old preschoolers attending traditional kindergartens.

Tab. 33 Comparison of the emotional abilities of preschool children according to the type of kindergartens they attend

	t	Sig. 2-tailed	Media Outdoor (N=54)	Traditional (N=54)
Assessments for item 1 '*Understands and talks about the consequences of his or her behavior and others*'	2,91	0.004	3,06	2,69
Assessments for item 2, '*Approaches new tasks with confidence*'	3,25	0.002	3,43	3,00
Assessments for item 3 '*Focused and resisting distraction*'	4,31	0.001	3,52	3,02
Assessments for item 4 '*Monitors his or her progress and seeks help accordingly*'	1,83	0.070	3,39	3,17
Assessments for item 5 '*Persistent in the face of difficulties*'	3,45	0.001	3,44	3,07
The degree of development of EMOTIONAL ABILITIES	4,46	0.001	2,98	2,69

Legend: t = value of t; sig. (2-tailed) = significance level of 5 % of t (confidence interval is 95 %)

The average assessments for *item 2* are significantly higher (t = 3.25, p. <0.01) for preschool children in outdoor kindergartens compared to traditional kindergartens. On average, 5-year-olds attending outdoor kindergartens approach new tasks with much more trust compared to 5-year-old preschoolers participating in traditional kindergartens.

The average assessments for *item 3* are significantly higher (t = 4.31, p. <0.01) for preschool children in outdoor kindergartens compared to traditional kindergartens. On average, 5-year-olds attending outdoor kindergartens are much more focused, resisting distraction far better compared to 5-year-old preschoolers participating in traditional kindergartens.

The average appreciation for *item 5* is significantly higher (t = 3.45, p. <0.01) for preschool children in outdoor kindergartens compared to traditional kindergartens. On average, 5-year-olds attending outdoor kindergartens are more persistent in the face of the more frequent difficulties compared to 5-year-old preschoolers attending traditional kindergartens.

The emotional abilities of children are significantly better developed (t = 4.46, p. <0.01) for preschool children attending outdoor kindergartens compared to those participating in traditional kindergartens.

In conclusion, since the *emotional abilities* of preschoolers participating in outdoor kindergartens are significantly more developed than those participating in traditional kindergartens, both as a whole (as a factor) and at the level of *some components related to behavioral consequences, addressing new tasks with confidence, focusing attention and persevering in the face of difficulties*, we can confirm the specific hypothesis 2.1.

III.7.2.2 Specific hypothesis 2.2

The *social skills* of 5-year-olds are significantly *more developed for preschool children in outdoor kindergartens* than those in traditional kindergartens.

In order to verify this hypothesis, the t test for independent samples was used *to measure whether the 5-year-old preschoolers' social skills* (referring both to the assessments for items 6–10 of the questionnaire and to the factor determined on their basis, the level of development of social skills) *are more statistically developed* in the case of children attending outdoor kindergartens (N = 54) compared to children attending traditional kindergartens (N = 54). The values, materiality thresholds of t, as well as the appreciation environments of preschoolers in the two subgroups are shown in Tab. 34.

For differences to be considered significant, the significance level of t (2-tailed) must be less than 0.05. The lower the significance level, the more significant the differences between subgroups are.

Analyzing the data in Tab. 34 above, we find that there are *significant differences* between preschoolers in outdoor and traditional kindergartens, both in terms of the *degree of development of their social skills* and as regards the *assessments of 4 out of 5 items* that make up this social factor.

Concerning the *components* of the emotional factor, we can see that there are significant differences depending on the type of kindergartens in which children participate in items *7, 8, 9 and 10*.

The average assessments for *item 7* are significantly higher (t = 4.41, p. <0.01) for preschool children in outdoor kindergartens compared to

Tab. 34 Comparison of the social skills of preschool children according to the kind of kindergartens they attend

	t	Sig. 2-tailed	Media	
			Outdoor (N=54)	Traditional (N=54)
Assessments for item 6 *'Negotiates when and how to fulfill a responsibility'*	1,28	0.203	2,87	2,69
Assessments for Item 7, *'Can solve social issues with colleagues by himself/herself'*	4,41	0.001	3,41	2,83
Assessments for item 8 *'Taught to be patient and to share things independently'*	2,92	0.004	3,37	3,02
Assessments for item 9 *'Engages in cooperative activities with colleagues independently'*	3,40	0.001	3,43	3,06
Assessments for item 10 *'Is aware of others' feelings and helps them feel comfortable'*	2,09	0.039	3,44	3,20
The degree of development of SOCIAL ABILITIES	5,12	0.001	2,96	2,59

Legend: t = value of t; sig. (2-tailed) = significance level of 5 % of t (confidence interval is 95 %)

traditional ones. On average, 5-year-old preschoolers participating in outdoor kindergartens can solve their social problems with their colleagues by themselves much more frequently than 5-year-old preschoolers participating in traditional kindergartens.

The average assessments for *item 8* is significantly higher (t = 2.92, p. <0.01) for preschool children in outdoor kindergartens compared to traditional ones. On average, 5-year-olds attending outdoor kindergartens have a lot more patience and share things more independently, compared to 5-year-old preschoolers participating in traditional kindergartens.

The average assessments for *item 9* is significantly higher (t = 3.40, p. <0.01) for preschool children in outdoor kindergartens compared to traditional ones. On average, 5-year-olds attending outdoor kindergartens engage in more independent activities with their colleagues compared to 5-year-old preschoolers participating in traditional kindergartens.

The average assessments for *item 10* is significantly higher (t = 2.09, p. <0.05) for preschool children in outdoor kindergartens compared to traditional ones. On average, 5-year-old preschool children participating in outdoor kindergartens are aware of the feelings of others and help them feel comfortable more frequently than 5-year-old preschoolers participating in traditional kindergartens.

The social skills of children are significantly better developed (t = 5.12, p. <0.01) for preschool children attending outdoor kindergartens compared to those participating in traditional kindergartens.

In conclusion, given that the *social skills* of preschoolers participating in outdoor kindergartens are significantly more developed than those participating in traditional ones, both as a whole (as a factor) and at *problem-solving components: social skills, patience, cooperation and empathy*, we can confirm the specific hypothesis 2.2.

III.7.2.3 Specific hypothesis 2.3

The *cognitive abilities* of 5-year-olds are significantly *more developed for preschool children in outdoor kindergartens* than in preschoolers in traditional kindergartens.

In order to verify this hypothesis, the t test for independent samples was used *to measure whether the 5-year-old preschoolers' cognitive abilities* (referring both to the assessments for items 11–17 of the questionnaire and to the factor determined on their basis, the level of development of emotional abilities) are more statistically significant for children attending outdoor kindergartens (N = 54) compared to children attending traditional kindergartens (N = 54). The values, significance thresholds of t and the assessment environments of preschoolers in the two subgroups are shown in Tab. 35.

For differences to be considered significant, the significance level of t (2-tailed) must be less than 0.05. The lower the significance level, the more significant the differences between subgroups are.

Analyzing the data in Tab. 35, we find that there are *significant differences* between preschoolers in outdoor kindergarten and those in traditional ones, both *in terms of the degree of development of their cognitive abilities* and in the *assessments of 4 out of 7 items* that make up this cognitive factor.

Tab. 35 Comparison of the cognitive abilities of preschool children according to the type of kindergartens they attend

	t	Sig. 2-tailed	Media Outdoor (N=54)	Traditional (N=54)
Assessments for item 11 'Is aware of his or her strengths and weaknesses'	3,98	0.001	3,26	2,78
Assessments for Item 12, 'Can communicate what he or she did or learned'	2,98	0.004	3,41	3,06
Assessments for item 13 'Can talk about future planned activities'	1,99	0.049	3,31	3,06
Assessments for item 14 'Can make choices and take motivated decisions'	0,30	0.762	3,31	3,28
Assessments for item 15 'Asks questions and suggests answers'	0,47	0.640	3,28	3,22
Assessments for item 16, 'Uses learning strategies previously taught'	0,89	0.376	3,31	3,22
Assessments for item 17, 'Adopts previously heard language for own purposes'	2,25	0.027	3,46	3,20
The degree of development of COGNITIVE ABILITIES	2,48	0.015	2,98	2,85

Legend: t = value of t; sig. (2-tailed) = significance level of 5 % of t (confidence interval is 95 %)

Concerning the *components* of the cognitive factor, we can see that there are significant differences depending on the type of kindergartens attend by children, in items *11, 12, 13 and 17*.

The average assessments for *item 11* is significantly higher (t = 3.98, p. <0.01) for preschool children in outdoor kindergartens compared to traditional ones. On average, 5-year-olds attending outdoor kindergartens are aware of their strengths and weaknesses to a greater extent compared to 5-year-old preschoolers participating in traditional kindergartens.

The average assessments for *item 12* is significantly higher (t = 2.98, p. <0.01) for preschool children in outdoor kindergartens compared to traditional ones. On average, 5-year-olds attending outdoor kindergarten can communicate about what they did or learn much more easily compared to 5-year-old preschoolers participating in traditional kindergartens.

The average rating for *item 13* is significantly higher (t = 1.99, p. <0.05) for preschool children in outdoor kindergartens compared to traditional ones. On average, 5-year-old preschool children participating in outdoor kindergartens can talk about future planned activities more easily, compared to 5-year-old preschoolers participating in traditional kindergartens.

The average appreciation for *item 17* is significantly higher (t = 2.25, p. <0.05) for preschool children in outdoor kindergartens compared to traditional ones. On average, 5-year-olds attending outdoor kindergartens adopt the language previously heard for their own purposes more frequently than 5-year-old preschoolers participating in traditional kindergartens.

The cognitive abilities of children are significantly better developed (t = 2.48, p. <0.05) for preschool children participating in outdoor kindergartens compared to those participating in traditional ones.

In conclusion, since the *cognitive abilities* of preschoolers participating in outdoor kindergartens are significantly more developed than those participating in traditional kindergartens, both as a whole (as a factor) and at the level of *components related to self-evaluation of strengths and weaknesses, the communication of learning, the expression of planned actions and the adaptation of language for own purposes*, we can confirm the specific hypothesis 2.3.

III.7.2.4 Specific hypothesis 2.4

The *motivational skills* of 5-year-olds are significantly *more developed in preschoolers in outdoor kindergartens* compared to preschool children in traditional kindergartens.

In order to verify this hypothesis, the t test for independent samples was used *to measure whether the motivational skills of 5-year-old preschoolers* (referring both to the assessments for items 18–22 of the questionnaire and to the factor determined on their basis, the degree of development of motivational skills) *are more statistically developed* in the case of children participating in outdoor kindergartens (N = 54) compared to children attending traditional kindergartens (N = 54). The values, significance thresholds of t, as well as the appreciation environments of preschoolers in the two subgroups are shown in Tab. 36.

Tab. 36 Comparison of the motivational abilities of preschool children according to the type of kindergartens in which they participate

	t	Sig. 2-tailed	Media Outdoor (N=54)	Traditional (N=54)
Assessments for item 18 *'Finds its own resources without the help of adults'*	3,49	0.001	3,28	2,83
Assessments for item 19 *'Develops own ways to perform tasks'*	1,70	0.092	3,39	3,19
Assessments for item 20, *'Initiatea activities'*	2,32	0.023	3,41	3,15
Assessments for Item 21, *'Planning own tasks, purpose and objectives'*	3,78	0.001	3,44	3,04
Assessments for item 22, *'Enjoys solving problems'*	1,79	0.077	3,50	3,28
The degree of development of **MOTIVATIONAL ABILITIES**	2,48	0.015	2,98	2,85

Legend: t = value of t; sig. (2-tailed) = significance level of 5 % of t (confidence interval is 95 %)

For differences to be considered significant, the significance level of t (2-tailed) must be less than 0.05. The lower the significance level, the more significant the differences between subgroups are.

Analyzing the data in Tab. 36, we find that there are *significant differences* between preschool children in outdoor and traditional kindergartens, both *in terms of the development of their motivational abilities* and as regards *the assessments of 3 out of 5 items* that make up this motivational factor.

Regarding *the components* of the emotional factor, we can see that there are significant differences depending on the type of kindergartens in which children participate in items 18, 20 and 21.

The average assessments for *item 18* is significantly higher (t = 3.49, p. <0.01) for preschool children in outdoor kindergartens compared to traditional ones. On average, 5-year-olds attending outdoor kindergartens find their own resources without the help of adults much more often compared to 5-year-old preschoolers participating in traditional kindergartens.

The average assessments for *item 20* is significantly higher (t = 2.32, p. <0.05) for preschool children in outdoor kindergartens compared to traditional ones. On average, 5-year-olds attending outdoor kindergartens initiate activities more frequently, compared to 5-year-old preschoolers participating in traditional kindergartens.

The average assessments for *item 21* is significantly higher (t = 3.78, p. <0.01) for preschool children in outdoor kindergartens compared to traditional ones. On average, 5-year-old preschool children participating in outdoor kindergartens plan their own tasks, goals and objectives more frequently than 5-year-old preschoolers participating in traditional kindergartens.

The motivational abilities of children are significantly better developed (t = 2.48, p. <0.05) for preschool children attending outdoor kindergartens compared to those participating in traditional ones.

In conclusion, since the *motivational skills* of preschools participating in outdoor kindergartens are significantly more developed than those participating in traditional ones, both as a whole (as a factor) and at the level of *some components related to finding their own resources, initiation of activities and planning of tasks*, we can confirm the specific hypothesis 2.4.

All the data analyzed in the specific hypotheses 2.1, 2.2, 2.3 and 2.4 lead to the *complete confirmation of the general hypothesis 2*, attesting to the fact that *all the 4 categories of emotional, social, cognitive and motivational abilities of 5-years-old preschoolers are more developed in the case of children participating in outdoor kindergartens* compared to those participating in traditional kindergartens.

In addition, *the significant differences in the type of kindergarten attended by preschool children* exist also at the level of the assessment of certain *items* of the questionnaire, components of the emotional, social, cognitive and motivational factors, as follows:

• *The emotional components related to the behavioral consequences (item 1), the approach of the new tasks with confidence (item 2), the focusing (item 3) and the persistence to the difficulties (item 5) are much more developed in the outdoor kindergarten preschoolers* compared to preschool children in traditional kindergartens;

- *Social components related to solving social problems* (item 7), *patience* (item 8), *cooperation* (item 9) *and empathy* (item 10) *are much more developed for outdoor kindergarten preschoolers* compared to preschool children in traditional kindergartens;
- *The cognitive components related to self-evaluation of strengths and weaknesses* (item 11), *learning to communicate* (item 12), *expressing planned actions* (item 13) *and adapting language for own purposes* (item 17) *are much more developed for outdoor kindergarten preschoolers* compared to preschool children in traditional kindergartens;
- *The motivational components related to finding own resources* (item 18), *initiation of activities* (item 20) *and task planning* (item 21) *are much more developed for outdoor kindergarten preschoolers* compared to preschool children in traditional kindergartens.

III.7.3 General hypothesis 3

There are statistically significant positive relationships between different categories of 5-year-old children's abilities.

This hypothesis refers to the *interdependence of the development of the four categories of abilities* of 5-year-old preschool children, respectively, emotional, social, cognitive and motivational skills. Since the specifics of the study are the comparative analysis of the preschool children's abilities in outdoor kindergartens (in the Czech Republic) and those from traditional kindergartens (in Romania), *we divided this general hypothesis into two specific hypotheses*, one dedicated to each subgroup of preschoolers, in part.

III.7.3.1 Specific hypothesis 3.1

The emotional, social, cognitive and motivational abilities of pre-school children in *outdoor kindergartens* correlate positively.

In order to verify the veracity of this hypothesis, we used the Pearson bivariate correlations to *determine the existence of statistically significant positive relationships between the degree of development of the four categories of emotional, social, cognitive and motivational abilities of children in outdoor kindergartens* (N = 54). The intercorrelations between the four categories of abilities are found in Tab. 37.

Tab. 37 Correlation of the development of the 4 categories of preschool children's skills in outdoor kindergartens

	Emotional abilities	Social abilities	Cognitive abilities	Motivational abilities
Emotional abilities	—	r = 0.456** p = 0.001	r = 0.428** p = 0.001	r = 0.382** p = 0.004
Social abilities	r = 0.456** p = 0.001	—	r = 0.510** p = 0.001	r = 0.658** p = 0.001
Cognitive abilities	r = 0.428** p = 0.001	r = 0.510** p = 0.001	—	r = 0.379** p = 0.005
Motivational abilities	r = 0.382** p = 0.004	r = 0.658** p = 0.001	r = 0.379** p = 0.005	—

Legend: r = value of the correlation coefficient; p = significance level of r
* = r is significant, having p <0.05 (probability of obtaining this correlation e <0.05);
** = r is very significant, having p <0.01 (probability of obtaining this correlation e <0.01)

For the relations to be considered significant, the significance level of r (2-tailed) must be less than 0.05. The lower the significance level, the more significant the relationship between the variables is.

Analyzing the correlations in Tab. 37, we note that all 4 skill categories correlate significantly with each other. All correlations are positive, which means that the scores of a factor increase as the scores of the other factor increase (they are directly proportional).

There is a *highly significant positive relationship between the degree of development of emotional abilities of preschool children in outdoor kindergartens and the degree of development of their abilities: social (r = 0.456, p <0.01), cognitive (r = 0.428, p < 0.01) and motivational (r = 0.382, p <0.01).* The more developed the emotional abilities of 5-year-old preschoolers in outdoor kindergartens are, the more their social, cognitive and motivational skills develop.

There is a *very significant positive relationship between the degree of development of the social abilities of preschool children in outdoor kindergartens and the degree of development of their abilities: emotional (r = 0.456, p <0.01), cognitive (r = 0.510, p < 0.01) and motivational (r = 0.658, p <0.01).* As the social skills of 5-year-old preschool children in kindergartens are more developed, their emotional, cognitive and motivational skills develop.

There is a *highly significant positive relationship between the degree of development of cognitive abilities of preschool children in outdoor kindergartens and the degree of development of their abilities: emotional (r = 0.428, p <0.01), social (r = 0.510, p < 0.01) and motivational (r = 0.379, p <0.01).* The more developed the cognitive skills of 5-year-old preschools in kindergartens are, the more their emotional, social and motivational skills develop.

There is a *highly significant positive relationship between the degree of development of the motivational abilities of preschool children in outdoor kindergartens and the degree of development of their abilities: emotional (r = 0.382, p <0.01), social (r = 0.658, p < 0.01) and cognitive (r = 0.379, p <0.01).* The more motivating the 5-year preschool skills in kindergartens are developing, the more their emotional, social and cognitive abilities develop.

Since all the abilities of 5-years-old preschool children in outdoor kindergartens correlate positively high with each other, we can confirm the specific hypothesis 3.1.

III.7.3.2 Specific hypothesis 3.2

The emotional, social, cognitive and motivational abilities of preschool children in *traditional kindergartens* are positively correlated.

In order to verify the veracity of this hypothesis, we used the Pearson binary correlations to determine the *existence of statistically significant positive relationships between the degree of development of the four categories of emotional, social, cognitive and motivational abilities of children in traditional kindergartens* (N = 54). The intercorrelations between the four categories of abilities are found in Tab. 38.

For relationships to be considered significant, the significance level of r (2-tailed) must be less than 0.05. The lower the significance level, the relationship between the variables is more significant.

Analyzing the correlations in Tab. 38, we note that three of the four categories of abilities are highly correlated with each other, namely emotional, cognitive and motivational abilities. All correlations are positive, which means that the scores of a factor increase with the increase of the scores of the other factor (they are directly proportional).

Tab. 38 Correlation of the development of the 4 categories of preschool children's skills in traditional kindergartens

	Emotional abilities	Social abilities	Cognitive abilities	Motivational abilities
Emotional abilities	—	r = 0.238 p = 0.084	r = 0.416** p = 0.002	r = 0.269* p = 0.049
Social abilities	r = 0.238 p = 0.084	—	r = −0.021 p = 0.878	r = 0.164 p = 0.236
Cognitive abilities	r = 0.416** p = 0.002	r = −0.021 p = 0.878	—	r = 0.346* p = 0.010
Motivational abilities	r = 0.269* p = 0.049	r = 0.164 p = 0.236	r = 0.346* p = 0.010	—

Legend: r = value of the correlation coefficient; p = significance level of r
* = r is significant, having p <0.05 (probability of obtaining this correlation e <0.05);
** = r is very significant, having p <0.01 (probability of obtaining this correlation e <0.01)

There is a *highly significant positive relationship between the degree of development of emotional abilities of preschool children in traditional kindergartens and the degree of development of their abilities: cognitive (r = 0.416, p <0.01) and motivational (r = 0.269, p <0.05).* The more developed the emotional abilities of 5-year-old preschoolers in traditional kindergartens are, the more their cognitive and motivational skills develop.

There is a *highly significant positive relationship between the degree of development of cognitive abilities of preschool children in traditional kindergartens and the degree of development of their abilities: emotional (r = 0.416, p <0.01) and motivational (r = 0.346, p <0.05).* The more developed the cognitive skills of 5-year-old preschoolers in traditional kindergartens are, the more their emotional and motivational abilities develop.

There is a *significant positive relationship between the degree of development of the motivational abilities of preschool children in traditional kindergartens and the degree of development of their abilities: emotional (r = 0.269, p <0.05) and cognitive (r = 0.346, p <0.05).* The more motivating the 5-year-old preschoolers in outdoor kindergarten's skills are developed, the more their emotional and cognitive skills develop.

Since most of the 5-year-old preschool children's abilities in the traditional kindergartens correlate positively high with each other, we can *partially confirm the specific hypothesis 3.2,* affirming that *only their emotional, cognitive and motivational abilities correlate positively.*

Considering the data analyzed, *we can also confirm the third general hypothesis of research,* namely the fact that there are statistically significant positive relationships between different categories of 5-year-old preschool children's abilities, as follows:

- Highly positive relationships between the development of the four categories of emotional, social, cognitive and motivational abilities of preschoolers participating in outdoor kindergartens;
- Significant positive relationships between the development of 3 categories of abilities, namely emotional, cognitive and motivational, of preschoolers participating in traditional kindergartens.

Conclusions

The purpose of this research was to determine whether outdoor kindergartens provide a 5-year-old preschool child with a better learning environment in terms of developing their emotional, social, cognitive and motivational skills compared to the traditional kindergarten learning environment.

It was assumed that there were *significant differences* in the level of development of the emotional, social, cognitive and motivational abilities of 5-year-old preschool children, depending on their *gender* and their *learning environment*, and the type of kindergarten they participate in. It is also assumed that there are *statistically significant positive relationships* between the different categories of abilities of 5-year-old children, both for outdoor and traditional kindergartens.

Thus, *three general research hypotheses* were formulated, each of them having more specific hypotheses.

For the purpose of collecting data to verify hypotheses, we used the Independent Learning Development Questionnaire (CHILD) 3–5, which was completed by 54 teachers of children attending outdoor kindergartens (in the Czech Republic) and 54 teacher educators of children participate in traditional kindergartens (from Romania).

All data collected using these tools was encoded, analyzed, processed and interpreted using the S.P.S.S. program.

Analyzing in comparison the four categories of preschool children in outdoor and traditional kindergartens, we noted the following aspects:

- Children's emotional abilities are well developed in the case of *98.15 % of preschool children attending outdoor kindergartens* and in the case of *68.52 % of preschool children participating in traditional kindergartens;*
- Children's social skills are well developed for *96.30 % of preschool children attending outdoor kindergartens* and *59.26 % of preschool children participating in traditional kindergartens;*

- Cognitive skills of children are well developed in the case of *98.15 %
  of preschool children attending outdoor kindergartens* and *85.19 % of
  preschool children participating in traditional kindergartens;*
- Motivational skills of children are well developed for *98.15 % of preschool children attending outdoor kindergartens* and *85.19 % of preschool children participating in traditional kindergartens.*

The results of the research were surprising, in the sense that all three
research hypotheses were confirmed, either in part or in full.

Regarding the first general hypothesis, *There are significant differences
in the level of development of 5 year preschool children's skills, depending
on their genre*, it contained four specific hypotheses pertaining to each
category of abilities. As a result of the analysis and interpretation of
the data, *significant differences in the development of gender abilities*
resulted only in children's social abilities, which are much more developed
for girls than for boys.

However, there were significant gender differences in some items of the
questionnaire (components of the skill factors), respectively, at the level of
certain *components: emotional*, related to behavioral consequences (item
1) and perseverance to difficulties (item 5); social issues related to negoti-
ation (item 6), social issues (item 7) and empathy (item 10) and a *motivational component* related to the enthusiasm of problem-solving (item 22).

Regarding the general hypothesis, *There are significant differences in
the level of development of 5-year-old children's skills, depending on
their learning environment, i.e., the type of kindergartens they participate in*, this has contained four specific hypotheses pertaining to each
category of abilities. After analyzing and interpreting the data, there
were *significant differences in the development of gender abilities* in all
4 categories of emotional, social and cognitive and motivational skills,
which were much more developed in the case of preschoolers in outdoor
kindergartens rather than of those in traditional kindergartens.

In addition, there were significant differences depending on the type
of kindergarten in which the children participate, in certain items of the
questionnaire (components of the skill factors), respectively, at the level of
certain *components: emotional*, related to the behavioral consequences
(item 1), the approach of the new tasks with confidence (item 2), power of

focus (item 3) and perseverance in the face of difficulties (item 5); *social,* connected to solving social issues (item 7), patience (item 8), cooperation (item 9) and empathy (item 10); *cognitive,* connected to self-evaluation of strengths and weaknesses (item 11), the communication of learning (item 12), the expression of planned actions (item 13) and the adaptation of the language for own purposes (item 17) and the *motivational,* related to finding own resources (item 18), initiating activities (item 20) and task planning (item 21).

Regarding the third general hypothesis, *There are statistically significant positive relationships between different skills of preschool children,* it included two specific hypotheses on interdependence skills in preschoolers in outdoor kindergartens, and the interdependence of skills in preschoolers in traditional kindergartens. Analysis and interpretation of data confirmed the existence of a highly significant positive correlation between the development of the four categories of emotional, social, cognitive and motivational skills of preschool children attending outdoor kindergartens, and the existence of significant positive correlations between the development of the three categories of skills, respectively, emotional, cognitive and motivational, of preschool children participating in traditional kindergartens. The confirmation of the two specific hypotheses led to the *confirmation of the third general hypothesis of research.*

The up-to-date researches highlighted the importance of the same-age children group, which at a certain stage becomes necessary to the child for its social apprenticeship. The group is the only place where he can compare himself and assess his abilities and limitations, form a more objective self-image, important premises in his ulterior integration into new groups and society (Shaffer & Kipp, 2014). It is very important that parents and kindergarten teachers understood and met the needs of preschool children's affective evolution. The persons with developed emotional abilities could be harmonious, more satisfied with their personal and professional life and communicate better with the others (Clipa & Gavriluta, 2017; A. Glava & C. Glava, 2002; Ştefan & Kallay, 2010; Tilea, Duţă & Reşceanu, 2017).The whole development processes of the people are saturated and influenced by the socialization processes. An increasing number of researchers indicate that by helping children develop effective social and emotional skills, they will achieve very good, long-term results in health and well-being (Lantieri, 2017) and highlight the role of each person in the development of entire society (Boyden & Levinson, 2000; Vrăsmaş, 2014).

The complex roles of outside activities in developing social and emotional competence were to be active and involved sectors in their own and community development. The emotional and social skills training should be the center of preschool children training, and the actual educational activities should take into account the results of the socio-emotional field, which are the beginning of the child's social life, its ability of establishing and maintaining interactions with adults and children (Children's well-being – adult's responsibility, 2014). All the evidence from research with this issues reveals the children are more growing up in nutrition, cognition, language, motor skills and socio-emotional competence and are more likely to engage in risky behaviors that result in school dropout, and violence in adolescence, and are less likely to become productive adults (Vegas, 2016).

In the current educational policies are underlined the influences of investments in Early Quality Education and are underlined the multiple effects on development of the personality and society (ECEA, 2019).

List of figures

List of tables

Bibliography

Ainsworth, M. D., Blehar, M. C., Waters, E. & Wall, S. (1978). *Patterns of Attachment: A Psychological Study of the Strange Situation.* Hillsdale, NJ: Lawrence Erlbaum Associates.

Alison, J. & James, A. (2008). *European Childhoods: Cultures, Politics and Childhoods in Europe.* London: Palgrave Macmillan.

Arvay, C. G. (2018). *The Biophilia Effect: A Scientific and Spiritual Exploration of the Healing Bond between Humans and Nature.* Boulder, CO: SoundsTrue.

Ashiabi, G. S. (2000). Promoting the emotional development of preschoolers. *Early Childhood Education Journal,* vol. 28, nr. 2, pp. 79–84.

Atwater, W. O. (1910). *Principles of Nutrition and Nutritive Value of Food.* Washington, DC: Government Printing Office.

Bagdascar, C. (1975). *Aspecte ale dezvoltării afectivității feminine.* București: Editura Didactică și Pedagogică.

Beaulieu, N. P. (2008). *Physical Activity and Children: New Research.* New York: Nova Science.

Birch, A. (2000). *Psihologia dezvoltării.* București: Ed. Tehnică.

Bisquerra, R. A. & Perez Escoda, N. (2007). Las competencias emotionales, vol. 10, *Educación XX1,* Faculty of Science of Education, Barcelona.

Booth, C., Rubin, K. & Krasmer, L. R. (1998). Perception of emotional support from mother and friend. *Child Development,* vol. 69, nr. 2, pp. 427–442.

Bowlby, J. (1969). *Attachment, Attachment and Loss.* Vol. I. New York: Basic Books.

Bowlby, J. (1980). *Loss, Sadness and Depression. Attachment and Loss.* Vol. III. New York: Basic Books.

Boyden, J. & Levison, D. (2000). *Children as Economic and Social Actors in the Development Process,* ECDI, Working Paper, nr. 1.

Bruce, T. (2012). *Early Childhood Practice: Froebel Today.* London: Sage.

Campbell, R., (2001). *Educația prin iubire*. București: Curtea Veche.

Carlson, E. (1998). A perspective longitudinal study of attachment. *Child Development*, vol. 699, nr. 44, pp. 1107–1128.

Cassidy, J. (2000). Child-mother attachment and the self in six-year-old. *Child Developments*, vol. 59, pp. 121–134.

Chen, A. (2019). From attachment to addiction: The mediating role of need satisfaction on social networking sites. *Computers in Human Behavior*, vol. 98, pp. 80–92, doi:10.1016/j.chb.2019.03.034

Chisholm, K. (1998). A three year follow-up attachment and indiscriminate friendliness in children adopted from Romanian orphanages. *Child Development*, vol. 69, nr. 4, pp. 1092–1106.

Ciofu, C. (1998). *Interacțiunea părinți – copii*. București: Ed. Amoltea.

Cîmpan, E. (2018). *WALDKINDERGARTEN – O legătură simbolică între trecut, prezent și viitor*. Brăila: Editura Sfântul Ierarh Nicolae.

Claparede, E. (1975). *Psihologia copilului și pedagogia experimentală*. București: Editura Didactică și Pedagogică.

Clipa, O. (2014a). Social and Emotional Development of Pre-schoolers. In *The actual Problems of the Theory and Practice of Modern Pre-School Education in Poland, Romania and Ukraine* (Coord. Otilia Clipa, Maria Oliznik si Malgoryata Stawiak-Ososinska). London: Ed. Lumen Media Publishing, pp. 19–33.

Clipa, O. (2014b). Transdisciplinarity and communicative action in multidimensional education. *Revista Romaneasca pentru Educatie Multidimensionala/Romanian Journal for Multidimensional Education*, Iasi: Lumen, vol. 6, nr. 2, pp. 9–13, http://dx.doi.org/10.18662/rrem/2014.0602.01.

Clipa, O. & Boghian, A. (2015). Stress factors and solutions for the phenomenon of burnout of preschool teachers. *Procedia – Social and Behavioral Sciences*, vol. 180, pp. 907–915, http://www.sciencedirect.com/science/article/pii/S1877042815015876

Clipa, O. & Gavriluta, P. (2017). Early Childhood Education – Parents Perceptions, *The European Proceedings of Social and Behavioural Sciences*, pp. 1716–1723. http://www.futureacademy.org.uk/publication/EpSBS/EduWorld2016PilestiRomania.

Clipa, O. & Schipor, D. M. (2015). Individual and Group Frames of Socialisation – the Relation between Collective Self-Esteem and Attachment Style. In *Educatia in societatea contemporana*. Iaşi: Lumen, pp. 65–75.

Dahlberg, G., Moss, P. & Pence, A. (1999). *Beyond Quality in Early Childhood Education and Care: Postmodern Perspectives*. London: Falmer Press.

De Canale, B. (2016). *Talenti e scuola dell'infanzia*. Napoli: Giapeto Editore.

Debesse M. (1981). *Etapele educaţiei în psihologia sec. XX*. Bucureşti: Editura Didactică şi Pedagogică.

Denham, S., Blair, K., DeMulder, E., Levitas, J., Sawyer, K. & Auerbach-Major, S. (2003). Preschool emotional competence: Pathway to social competence? *Child Development*, vol. 74, nr. 1, pp. 238–256, https://doi.org/10.1111/1467-8624.00533.

Dell Rosso, S. (2010). *Waldkindergarten: Ein pädagogisches Konzept mit Zukunft?* Hamburg: Diplomica Verlag GmbH.

Delors J. (coord.) (2000). *Comoara lăuntrică*. Iaşi: Polirom.

Dirtu, C. (2016). Stilurile de atasament si eficienta actului educational in copilarie. In Stan, L. (eds.). *Educatia timpurie, Probleme si solutii*. Iasi: Polirom, pp. 150–158.

Dumbrava, A. (2016). *Premise neurobiologice ale educatiei timpurii, Dezvoltarea copilului si educatia timpurie* (Stan, L. eds). Iasi: Polirom, pp. 36–74.

Durastanti, F., de Santis, C., Orefice, G., Paolini, S. & Rizzuto, M. (2016). *Agrinidi, agriasili e asili nel bosco: Nuovi percorsi educativi nella natura*. Firenze: Editrice Aam Terra Nuova.

Elias, M., Tobias, S. & Friendlander, B. (2007). *Inteligenta emotionala in educatia copiilor*. Bucuresti: Curtea Veche.

Elovainio, M., Jokela, M., Rosenström, T., Pulkki-Râbäck, L., Hakulinen, C., Josefsson, K., Hintsanen, M., Hintsa, T., Raitakari, O.T. & Keltikangas-Järvinen, L. (2015). Temperament and depressive symptoms: What is the direction of the association? *Journal of Affective Disorders*, vol. 170, pp. 203–212.

Erikson, E. (1968). *The life Cycle Completed*. New York: Norton.

Erikson, E. (2015). *Copilărie şi societate*. Bucureşti: Trei.

European Commission/EACEA/Eurydice. (2019). *Eurydice Brief: Key Data on Early Childhood Education and Care in Europe.* Luxembourg: Publications Office of the European Union, https://eacea.ec.europa.eu/national-policies/eurydice/content/eurydice-brief-key-data-early-childhood-education-and-care-europe_en.

Flynn, S., Noone, C. & Sarma, K. M. (2018). An exploration of the link between adult attachment and problematic Facebook use. *BMC Psychology*, vol. 6, nr. 1, p. 34.

Foran, A., Redmond, K. & Loeffler, T. A. (2016). The *get – Outside Guide to Winter Activities.* Champaign, IL: Human Kinetics.

Fröbel, F. (1826). *Die Menschenerziehung, die Erziehungs-, Unterrichts-, und Lehrkunst.* Leipzig: Verlag der allgemeinen deutschen Erziehungsanstalt.

Giallongo, A. (1990). *Il bambino medievale: Educazione ed infanzia nel Medioevo.* Bari: edizioni Dedalo.

Gilbertson, K., Bates, T., McLaughlin, T. & Ewert, A. (2006). *Outdoor Education: Methods and Strategies.* Champaign, IL: Human Kinetics.

Glava, A. & Glava, C. (2002). *Introducere în pedagogia preşcolară.* Cluj-Napoca: Ed. Dacia Educaţional.

Gluschkoff, K., Oksman, E., Knafo-Noam, A., Dobewall, H., Hintsa, T., Keltikangas-Järvinen, L., et al. (2018). The early roots of compassion: from child care arrangements to dispositional compassion in adulthood. *Personality and Individual Differences*, vol. 129, pp. 28–32. doi:10.1016/j.paid.2018.03.005.

Goleman, D. (2007). *Social Intelligence: The New Science of Human Relationship.* New York: Ed. Bantam Dell.

Golu, F. (2009). *Joc şi învăţare la copilul preşcolar. Ghid pentru educatori, părinţi şi psihologi.* Bucureşti: EDP.

Greene, S. & Hogan, D. (2005). *Researching children's experience.* London: SAGE. doi:10.4135/9781849209823.

Guillaud, F. & Lemoine, M. (2008). *Philosophie Tles L, ES et S: Auteurs et concepts.* Bréal.

Hart, B. & Risley, T. (2013). The Early Catastrophic. *Educational Review*, vol. 17, pp. 110–118.

Hintsanen, M., Lipsanen, J., Pulkki-Råback, L., Kivimäki, M., Hintsa, T. & Keltikangas-Järvinen, L. (2009). EAS temperaments as predictors of unemployment in young adults: A 9-year follow-up of the cardiovascular risk in young Finns study. *Journal of Research in Personality*, vol. 43, pp. 618–623. doi:10.1016/j.jrp.2009.03.013.

Howe, N. & Recchia, H. (2006). Sibling Relations and Their Impact on Children's Development. In *Encyclopedia on Early Childhood Development*. Montreal, Quebec: Centre of Excellence for Early Childhood Development, pp. 1–7.

Iacob, L. (1999). Dezvoltarea cognitivă şi educaţia intelectuală. *Învăţământului preşcolar*, nr. 1–4, Bucureşti.

Ignat, A. A. (2011). *Consilierea pentru dezvoltarea socială şi emoţională a copiilor cu aptitudini înalte*. Bucureşti: EDP.

Ingold, T. (2000). *The Perception of the Environment: Essays on livelihood, dwelling and skill*. London/New York: Routledge/Taylor & Francis Group.

Jenks, C. (2005). *Childhood: Critical Concepts in Sociology*, Vol. 1. London/New York: Routledge/Taylor & Francis Group.

Kirrane, M., Kilroy, S., Kidney, R., Flood, P. & Bauwens, R. (2019). The relationship between attachment style and creativity: The mediating roles of LMX and TMX. *European Journal of Work and Organizational Psychology*, https://doi.org/10.1080/13594 32X.2019.1646247.

Kjørholt, A. T. & Qvortrup, J. (2012). *The Modern Child and the Flexible Labour Market: Early Childhood Education and Care*. London: Palgrave Macmillan.

Knight, S. (2011). *Risk & Adventure in Early Years Outdoor Play: Learning from Forest Schools*. London: SAGE.

Knight, S. (2013). *International Perspectives on Forest School: Natural Spaces to Play and Learn*. London: SAGE.

Kobak, R. R., Cole, H. E., Ferenz-Gillies, R., Fleming, W. S. & Gamble, W. (1993). Attachment and emotion regulation during mother-teen problem solving: A control theory analysis. *Child Development*, vol. 64, nr. 1, pp. 231–245.

Kreher, A. (2008). *Der Waldkindergarten: Ein Neues Konzept der Vorschulpädagogik*. Grin Verlag GmbH.

Lantieri, L. (2017). *Dezvoltarea inteligenţei emoţionale a copiilor. Tehnici de a cultiva puterea lăuntrică a copiilor (Building Emotional*

Intelligence: Techniques to Cultivate Inter Stregth in Children). Bucureşti: Ed. Curtea Veche.

Lee A. & Hankin, B. L. (2009). Insecure attachment, dysfunctional attitudes, and low self-esteem predicting prospective symptoms of depression and anxiety during adolescence. *Journal of Clinical Child & Adolescent Psychology*, vol. 38, pp. 219–231. doi:10.1080/15374410802698396.

Liu, C. & Ma, J. L. (2019). Adult attachment style, emotion regulation, and social networking sites addiction. *Frontiers in Psychology*, vol. 10, p. 2352. doi:10.3389/fpsyg.2019.02352.

Locke, J. (1841). *An Essay Concerning Human Understanding*. London: Printed for Thomas Tegg, Cheapside.

Locke, J. (2007). *Quelques pensées sur l'éducation*. Paris: Librairie Philosophique J. Vrin.

Lopez, F. G., Gover, M. R., Leskela, J., Sauer, E. M., Schirmer, L. & Wyssmann, J. (1997). Attachment styles, shame, guilt, and collaborative problem-solving orientations. *Personal Relationships*, vol. 4, nr. 2, pp. 187–199.

Lorber, K. (2012). *Erziehung und Bildung von Kleinkindern: Historische. Entwicklungen und elementar pädagogischen Handlungskonzepte*. Hamburg: Diplomica Verlag GmbH.

Malim, T., Birch, A. & Hayward, S. (2000). *Psihologia dezvoltării*. Bucureşti: Ed. Tehnică.

Malouff, J. M., Thorsteinsson, E. B. & Schutte, N. S. (2005). The relationship between the five-factor model of personality and symptoms of clinical disorders: A meta-analysis. *Journal of Psychopathology and Behavioral Assessment*, vol. 27, pp. 101–114. doi:10.1007/s10862-005-5384-y.

MEN (2008). *Curriculum pentru educaţia timpurie a copiilor de la 3 la 6/7 ani*. documente MEN.

Miklitz, I. (2000). *Der Waldkindergarten: Dinensionen eines pädagogischen Ansatzes*. Neuwied: Luchterhand.

Montessori, M. (1948). *The Discovery of the Child*. Adyar, Madras, India: Kalakshetra..

Montessori, M. (2002). *The Montessori Method*. Mineola, NY: Dover.

Norwegian Directorate for Education and Training. (2014). *Children's Well-being – Adult's Responsibility*. Oslo: UDIR.

Oksman, E., Rosenström, T., Gluschkoff, K., Saarinen, A., Hintsanen, M., Pulkki-Råback, L., ... Keltikangas-Järvinen, L. (2019). Associations between early childcare environment and different aspects of adulthood sociability: The 32-year prospective young Finns study. *Frontiers in Psychology*, vol. 10, p. 2060. doi:10.3389/fpsyg.2019.02060.

Oliverio, A. & Oliverio Ferraris, A. (2011). *A Piedi Nudi Nel Verde; Giocare per imparare a vivere*. Firenze: Giunti Editore S.p.A.

Opre, A. (coord.) (2010). *Lumea lui Self. Poveşti pentru dezvoltarea socio-emoţională a copiilor preşcolari*. Cluj-Napoca: Editura ASCR.

Osterrieth, P. (1976). *Introducere în psihologia copilului*. Bucureşti: E.D.P.

Panfile, T. & Deborah, L. (2012). Attachment security and child's empathy: The mediating role of emotion regulation. *Merrill-Palmer Quarterly*, vol. 58, nr. 1, pp. 1–21. Published by Wayne State University Press. doi:10.1353/mpq.2012.0003.

Pavelcu, V. (1969). *Viaţa sentimentelor*. Bucureşti: Editura Didactică şi Pedagogică.

Petrovai, D. & Petrica, S. (2013). *Cum îi ajutăm pe copii să meargă fericiţi la şcoală*. Bucureşti: Miniped.

Petrovai, D., Preda, V., Petrica, S. & Brănişteanu, R. (2012). *Pentru un copil sănătos emoţional şi social. Ghid practic pentru educatorul care construieşte încredere*. Piteşti: V&I Integral.

Piaget, J. (1976). *Construirea realului la copil*. Bucureşti: E.D.P.

Piaget, J. & Inhelder, B. (1969). *Psihologia copilului*. Bucureşti: Editura Didactică şi Pedagogică.

Rank, M. (2004). *Stärken und Schwächen des neunen Vorschulpädagogik- Konzeptes Waldkindergarten aus Sicht der MitarbeiterInnen*. Grin Verlag.

Rath, N. & Ravenberg, K. (2001). *Der schulkindergarten. Band 2: Neue Arbeitsmodelle*. Münster/New York/Berlin: Waxmann.

Richards, C. & Taylor Philip, H. (1998). *How Shall We School Our Children? Primary Education and Its Future*. Bristol, PA: Falmer Press/Taylor & Francis.

Richards, D. A. & Hackett, R. D. (2012). Attachment and emotion regulation: Compensatory interactions and leader-member exchange. *Leadership Quarterly*, vol. 23, nr. 4, pp. 686–701.

Rizzolatti, G. & Craighero, L. (2004). The mirror-neuron system. *Annual Review of Neuroscience*, vol. 27, pp. 169–192.

Rocco, M. (2000). *Creativitate şi inteligenţă emoţională*. Iaşi: Polirom.

Rose, D. (2014). *It's Not about the Broccoli: Three Habits to Teach Your Kids for a Lifetime of Healthy Eating.* New York: Penguin Group.

Rousseau, J. J. (1979). *Emile or on Education*. Introduction, Translation and Notes by Allan Bloom. New York: Basic Books.

Sax, L. (2007). *Boys Adrifts: The Five Factors Driving the Growing Epidemic of on Unmotivated Boys and Underachieving Young Men*, New York: Basic Books.

Schulthess, D. (1996). *La nature: thèmes philosophiques, thèmes d'actualitè*. Actes du XXVe Congrès de l'Association des sociétés de philosophie de langue française (ASPLF), Lausanne, Revue de théologie et de philosophie, Lausanne (Suisse).

Shaffer, D. R. & Kipp, K. (2014). *Developmental Psychology: Childhood and Adolescence* (9th ed.). Belmont, CA: Wadsworth Cengage Learning.

Sobel, D. (2016). *Nature Preschools and Forest Kindergartens: The Handbook for Outdoor Learning.* St. Paul, MN: Redleaf Press.

Sofo, A. & Calabrese, F. (2015). *Nuovi contesti di apprendimento tra tradizione ed innovazione: agrinido e agriasilo.* Lulu Book Company.

Stewart, R. B. (1983). Sibling attachment relationships: Child–infant interaction in the strange situation. *Developmental Psychology*, vol. 19, nr. 2, pp. 192–199. https://doi.org/10.1037/0012-1649.19.2.192.

Suzuki, H. & Tomoda, A. (2015). Roles of attachment and self-esteem: impact of early life stress on depressive symptoms among Japanese institutionalized children. *BMC Psychiatry*, vol. 15, nr. 1, p. 8.

Şchiopu, U. (1967). *Psihologia copilului*. Bucureşti: Editura Didactică şi Pedagogică.

Şchiopu, U. (1997). Dezvoltarea sociabilităţii la copilul preşcolar. *Învăţământul preşcolar*, nr. 3–4, pp. 647–650, Bucureşti.

Ştefan, C. & Kallay, E. (2010). *Dezvoltarea competenţelor emoţionale şi sociale la preşcolari – Ghid practice pentru părinţi.* Cluj-Napoca: Ed ASCR.

Teodorescu, R. (1999).Socializarea copilului prin joc. *Învăţământul preşcolar*, nr. 1–2.

Tilea, M., Duţă, O.-A. & Reşceanu, A. (eds.) (2017). *Sustainable and Solidary Education. Reflections and Practices.* Frankfurt am Main: Peter Lang.

Vegas, E. (eds.) (2016). *Education and Early Childhood Development Sector Framework* [Public Document]. http://idbdocs.iadb.org/ wsdocs/getdocument.aspx?docnum=40398589.

Verza, E. & Verza, F. E. (2017). *Psihologia copilului.* Bucureşti: Trei.

Vrăşmaş, E. (1999). *Educaţia copilului preşcolar.* Bucureşti: Editura ProHumanitate.

Vrăşmaş, E. (2014). *Educaţia timpurie.* Bucureşti: Ed. Arlequin.

Wallon, H. (1978). *Evoluţia psihologică a copilului.* Bucureşti: E.D.P.

Warden, C. (2015). *Learning with Nature: Embedding Outdoor Practice.* London: SAGE.

Weiner, I. & Craighead, W. E. (eds.) (2010). *The Corsini Encyclopedia of Psychology.* Vol. 4. Wiley.

Worsley J. D., Mansfield, R. & Corcoran, R. (2018). Attachment anxiety and problematic social media use: The mediating role of well-being. *Cyberpsychology & Behavior*, vol. 21, pp. 563–568. 10.1089/ cyber.2017.0555.

ERZIEHUNGSKONZEPTIONEN UND PRAXIS

Herausgeben von Gerd-Bodo von Carlsburg

Band 21 Bernd Arnold: Medienerziehung und moralische Entwicklung von Kindern. Eine medienpädagogische Untersuchung zur Moral im Fernsehen am Beispiel einer Serie für Kinder im Umfeld der Werbung. 1993.

Band 22 Dimitrios Chatzidimou: Hausaufgaben konkret. Eine empirische Untersuchung an deutschen und griechischen Schulen der Sekundarstufen. 1994.

Band 23 Klaus Knauer: Diagnostik im pädagogischen Prozeß. Eine didaktisch-diagnostische Handreichung für den Fachlehrer. 1994.

Band 24 Jörg Petersen / Gerd-Bodo Reinert (Hrsg.): Lehren und Lernen im Umfeld neuer Technologien. Reflexionen vor Ort. 1994.

Band 25 Stefanie Voigt: Biologisch-pädagogisches Denken in der Theorie. 1994.

Band 26 Stefanie Voigt: Biologisch-pädagogisches Denken in der Praxis. 1994.

Band 27 Reinhard Fatke / Horst Scarbath: Pioniere Psychoanalytischer Pädagogik. 1995.

Band 28 Rudolf G. Büttner / Gerd-Bodo Reinert (Hrsg.): Naturschutz in Theorie und Praxis. Mit Beispielen zum Tier-, Landschafts- und Gewässerschutz. 1995.

Band 29 Dimitrios Chatzidimou / Eleni Taratori: Hausaufgaben. Einstellungen deutscher und griechischer Lehrer. 1995.

Band 30 Bernd Weyh: Vernunft und Verstehen: Hans-Georg Gadamers anthropologische Hermeneutikkonzeption. 1995.

Band 31 Helmut Arndt / Henner Müller-Holtz (Hrsg.): Schulerfahrungen – Lebenserfahrungen. Anspruch und Wirklichkeit von Bildung und Erziehung heute. Reformpädagogik auf dem Prüfstand. 2. Aufl. 1996.

Band 32 Karlheinz Biller: Bildung erwerben in Unterricht, Schule und Familie. Begründung – Bausteine – Beispiele. 1996.

Band 33 Ruth Allgäuer: Evaluation macht uns stark! Zur Unverzichtbarkeit von Praxisforschung im schulischen Alltag. 1997. 2., durchges. Aufl. 1998.

Band 34 Christel Senges: Das Symbol des Drachen als Ausdruck einer Konfliktgestaltung in der Sandspieltherapie. Ergebnisse aus einer Praxis für analytische Psychotherapie von Kindern und Jugendlichen. 1998.

Band 35 Achim Dehnert: Untersuchung der Selbstmodelle von Managern. 1997.

Band 36 Shen-Keng Yang: Comparison, Understanding and Teacher Education in International Perspective. Edited and introduced by Gerhard W. Schnaitmann. 1998.

Band 37 Johann Amos Comenius: Allverbesserung (Panorthosia). Eingeleitet, übersetzt und erläutert von Franz Hofmann. 1998.

Band 38 Edeltrud Ditter-Stolz: Zeitgenössische Musik nach 1945 im Musikunterricht der Sekundarstufe I. 1999.

Band 39 Manfred Luketic: Elektrotechnische Lernsoftware für den Technikunterricht an Hauptschulen. 1999.

Band 40 Gerhard Baltes / Brigitta Eckert: Differente Bildungsorte in systemischer Vernetzung. Eine Antwort auf das Problem der funktionellen Differenzierung in der Kooperation zwischen Jugendarbeit und Schule. 1999.

Band 41 Roswit Strittmatter: Soziales Lernen. Ein Förderkonzept für sehbehinderte Schüler. 1999.

Band 42 Thomas H. Häcker: Widerstände in Lehr-Lern-Prozessen. Eine explorative Studie zur pädagogischen Weiterbildung von Lehrkräften. 1999.

www.peterlang.com